Truffles

Truffles

ELISABETH LUARD

PHOTOGRAPHS BY JOHN HESELTINE

FRANCES LINCOLN

For Nicholas, who loved a truffle baked with cream

Frances Lincoln Ltd
4 Torriano Mews
Torriano Avenue
London NW5 2RZ
www.franceslincoln.com

British Library Cataloguing-in-Publication Data
A catalogue record for this book is available from the British Library.

First Frances Lincoln Edition 2006

ISBN 0-7112-2493-5
ISBN 978-0-7112-2493-3

Conceived, edited and designed for Frances Lincoln by
Berry & Co (Publishing) Ltd
47 Crewys Road
Childs Hill
London NW2 2AU

Edited by Susan Berry
Designed and illustrated by Anne Wilson
Index compiled by Marie Lorimer

Printed and bound in Singapore by Tien Wah Press Pte. Ltd.

9 8 7 6 5 4 3 2 1

Contents

INTRODUCTION

How does a rational person, accustomed to the daily business of cooking for a family, manage to fall in love with a subterranean fungus that looks like a lump of roughly cracked earth, smells like nothing you'd wish to describe in polite company, and has no measurable worth as a foodstuff apart from a few minerals and a little fibre?

It happens.

It happened to me one bright day in winter in the uplands of Provence, in the company of an elderly gentleman, to whom I had only just been introduced, and a small black dog called Noirot. Everyone who falls in love with the truffle has a similar tale to tell. There's a place and person, and a canine, which, though infrequently these days, might sometimes be a pig. This is no coincidence. While many have tasted the truffle in an inferior state — as little black specks in the pâté, or (better) in the form of translucent threads grated of over a mound of buttery pasta — these experiences are nothing compared to the moment you dig up your own.

After that, it's an affair of the heart. Nothing else can explain the passion with which its admirers pursue the object of desire, scrabbling in the earth or emptying the purse — whatever it takes to hold it in the hand, to smell, to taste, to savour. No other substance in the gastronomic firmament, however fragrant or rare, or exquisite, or unobtainable, arouses such strong emotions.

Let me put the case for treasuring the truffle. Leaving aside culinary considerations, the truffle is not just a fragrance, a flavour, a face — though all these things contribute to its allure — it's a nugget of vegetable matter searching, as must all living things, for a niche in which it can thrive. And its niche is remarkably specific. Let one thing fall out of line, and the whole enterprise falters and fails.

The odds are weighted heavily against its survival. As a semi-parasite — symbiotic, but only up to a point, since it stunts the growth of the trees on which it depends — its needs are inconveniently specific. Once it has managed to find and colonize the hair-fine roots of its host-plant in soil that has the right degree of porosity, in a situation in which the climate suits its fruiting-cycle, it needs a

If music be the food of love . . . the local brass band at Aqualagna in Le Marche, playing in the National Fair of the White Truffle, which takes place there every October.

spore-spreader. As a subterranean fungus, it needs to attract the attention of a creature capable of digging it up, eating it and excreting it into an environment in which it can thrive. Wild pigs, bears, hedgehogs, squirrels, badgers and other omnivorous creatures of the wildwoods served as vehicles for its spores, as indeed did our ancestors, forest-hunters and plain-scourers who lived much as other mammals, spreading their debris round their territories.

For the truffle, the arrangement worked perfectly well as long as the forests were there for the colonizing. Once the trees began to fall to the woodsman's axe, the creatures that depended on wildwood were obliged to alter their habits or continued to exist only through domestication: pigs were moved to styes, cattle to fields, sheep to folds. And humankind, begetter of all these changes, developed sophisticated social habits which, in due course, led to the need for plumbing – removing, at a stroke, its usefulness as a spore-spreader. What was the truffle to do? No need for panic. While humankind has a short-sighted habit of ridding the planet of anything it thinks it doesn't need, it also has the means to improve the chances of anything it likes.

Survival is a risky business even for the earth's most visible predator: a tidal wave and we're drowned, a shrug of the earth's crust and we're crushed, a belch of its innards and we're done to a crisp. What chance, therefore, has a subterranean fungus dependent on having its spores spread by mammal-power and which has turned over the management of its life-cycle to its vegetable host?

Look more closely, however, and you'll observe that the truffle has carved itself a niche – social, political, cultural – designed to appeal to the only creature on the planet capable of ensuring its success. As the earth's sole cultivator – well, leaving aside certain breeds of ant – we can do as we choose. We can uproot the natural truffle grounds or we can leave their host-plants untended and vulnerable, either way condemning them to vanish along with other flotsam which makes up the planet's diversity, but for which we see no obvious need. Or, instead, we can encourage their proliferation because we like to eat them, and are prepared to pay good money for the privilege. Good money is the key. It buys the interest of scientists, land for planting in such a way as to produce results, and (once the money has been spent) a willingness to wait. Not bad for an organism that lacks measurable intelligence.

In modern times, the strategy has proved remarkably successful. Truffles produced under cultivation now provide the major part – around 70 per cent – of the world's marketable crop. As a crop, the truffle marks the borderline where wilderness ends and cultivation begins. Neither truly wild nor truly cultivated, it can be encouraged but not coerced to fruit. Once established, it holds a mirror to those complex changes that can only otherwise be measured by chemists — but even then without the truffle's unerring accuracy. It can tell us, by appearing or failing to appear, whether the ground it seeds is as it always was, whether the earth is over-stimulated or impoverished, or if the run-off from field and hedge is healthy or sick, or if rain which stimulates its growth is acid or clean. At its simplest, it can tell us if the sun is in its heaven and all's right with the world.

As an ecological indicator — the botanical equivalent of the miner's canary, the caged bird whose singing or lack of it served to warn the worker at the coal-face of trouble ahead — the truffle will tell us all we need to know about what's happening below, above and on the surface of the planet. And a world in which the truffle cannot thrive is a world in which the soil from which we draw our sustenance no longer functions as it should. Air, water, earth — even fire itself in the form of the sun — all must combine to produce the miracle of the truffle's fruiting. And if the crop thrives we need to know why. And if it fails, we have only ourselves to blame.

The magic of the truffle — why it appears in some places and not in others, its relatives, cousins and brothers, its biological make-up, methods of artificial production, strategies for husbandry — is under constant scrutiny. In a world hungry for new experiences, truffles are big business. Hundreds of books — serious, practical, romantic — are written about it, hundreds of websites devoted to it. Even so, its allure remains mysterious, its attraction undefinable.

It's astonishingly valuable. In an ordinary year, a kilo of the white truffle of Italy (found in seven of the most northerly provinces and nowhere else on the planet), fetches a market price of some 6,000 euros, the price of a small car. A black French truffle of equivalent weight — to my mind its equal in gastronomic value, though less rare — costs around 2,000.

The history and literature of the truffle goes back to the Romans; indeed there are records of truffles as far back as the Greeks though these are thought to refer to members of the related *Terfezia* species, sand-buried desert truffles, which, though less valued outside their lands of origin, continue to fetch good prices in the souk.

There are truffles on every continent: some good to eat, some exquisite, some of lesser interest, some of no gastronomic value whatsoever. There are truffles for all conditions and all climates — wet or dry, hot or cool. Mankind's taste for it is ancient: truffle-debris is found in stone-age middens. Hunter-gathers appreciated its worth. In David Livingstone's account of his Christian mission in southern Africa there's a record of an enormous "desert" truffle found by San tribesmen, the original inhabitants of the Kalahari wilderness. These days, gourmets cross continents just to taste it, restauranteurs pay ridiculous prices to secure the largest and most perfect (and then, like as not, fail to understand the prize must be consumed as soon as purchased).

Truffles are creatures of place, taking their fragrance, texture, colour, shape and size not only from their host-plant but from the earth in which they're formed. And even when the species and land of origin is shared, experts will tell you no single truffle ever tastes exactly like any other. Such variations might seem impossible until you talk to the dealers who judge individual worth. For chefs whose patrons rate presentation above substance, the black truffle (*Tuber melanosporum*) has the added advantage of visibility even in small quanties — never mind the fragrance, smell the money. In addition, the black, unlike the white, takes well to the application of heat, making it suitable for the elaborate cooked dishes admired by their employers, the men who pay the bills. This may, to some degree, explain why the black is admired to the exclusion of all others in France, while the white excites similar feelings in Italy (except in the region of Norcia, where the black is equally valued).

For the novice, the first truffle, newly released from its bed of earth, is an emotional moment — but it's not yet love. The experience slips into memory, and there it stays, dormant in the recesses of the mind until reawakened, perhaps by chance, by a dish in a restaurant or a return to that place where truffles can be enjoyed at their moment of perfection. From that moment on, a single sniff is enough to liberate memories of every other moment when truffles were tasted.

And it's this, the ability to linger in the mind long after the flavour is forgotten, which makes the tuber so precious. Memory never has so much power as when transmitted through the flavour of a foodstuff that has been consumed for pleasure ever since someone first noticed that bison tastes better when roasted in its jacket. The truffle has, too, an astonishing ability to transmit its perfume to other foodstuffs, seeping through the porous shells of fresh eggs when left alone with a basketful overnight; when slivered over a tangle of home-made pasta; when roasted with a fillet of pork or slipped into a sauce for steak;

or when inserted delicately beneath the skin of a *poulet de Bresse*; or even when, quite simply, roasted in a jacket of bread-dough when the day's baking is done.

And if you think yourself immune to its charms, the probability is you've not been in the right place at the right time. Of the two species by which all others are judged — *Tuber melanosporum* and *T. magnatum* — both are native to the Mediterrean's woodlands. The season runs from December to March for *T. melanosporum* (the Périgord black) and from the first of October to the last of November for *T. magnatum* (the Piedmont white). Of other native European species of comparable fragrance, May to December is the season for the summer truffle (*T. aestivum*). The black-skinned Burgundy truffle (*T. uncinatum*) overlaps with the summer truffle from early October until end December. The little white truffle (*T. borchii*, also known as "*bianchetto*"), arrives in Italian markets in mid-January, when it looks, though smaller, much like the Piedmont white, although its season never overlaps. In France, the black musk truffle (*Tuber brumale*), is in the market at the same time as the Périgord black, for which it can, though inferior, be mistaken. Desert truffles of the genus *Terfezia* come into the market in the lands of Arabia immediately after the spring rains, from February to April. New World truffles, notably the Oregon truffle (*T. gibbosum*), and the Texan truffle (*T. texensis*) fruit at other times: local knowledge will set you right, always remembering that a truffle out of season is, well, a truffle in an inferior state.

Meanwhile, for all that we know about it now and the discoveries we may yet make, the appeal of the truffle remains elusive, not least because of its complexity — social and moral as well as gastronomic. Its reputation has suffered not one whit from the chemists' scrutiny — study that has allowed the identification of the elements that deliver its scent. Even the appearance of apparently limitless quantities of look-alikes and second-bests cannot dent its value, since a crop once harvested by the poor and sold to the rich becomes available to all. And if the experience these substitutes provide is not as perfect as it should be: once you know a little of what you're missing, you'll want the real thing. Like the perfect love-affair, you'll know it when you find it. And then, forget the little flirtations, this is for real — a passion which lasts a lifetime.

Meet the truffle

Erotic, earthy, astonishingly sexy, exquisite, smouldering, penetrating, intense, heavenly compound of hashish, essence of opium – it can't all be in the mind. Or can it?

And if the appeal of the merchandise is not immediately obvious, a bit of acting will do the trick. On a visit in October 2004 to the annual white truffle-fest at Sant'Agata Feltria, one of Italy's more remote truffle-towns in a mountainous corner of the Emiglia Romagna, I was in the process of negotiating the price of a modest little nugget when the seller lifted the ivory globe to his nostrils, inhaled dramatically and – glancing at my companion (male) – raised his eyes to heaven. No further sales-pitch required. Sold to the lady with the handbag.

Even those who are passionate about truffles can't explain their passion. There's plenty of talk of black diamonds and ivory princesses – but it's the subtext that counts. And when we finally reach out for what it really tells us, having reached it, we drop it like a hot potato. Flirtatious or coquettish is one thing, tousled sheets of a brothel are quite another. There's talk of chocolate and lavender, and wet autumnal woods – but none of these come close to explaining its oddity. It smells, you finally have to admit, like nothing else on earth. Like the durian, that other forbidden fruit whose foetid fragrance gets people thrown out of public places, it repels as easily as it attracts. If you carry

Black truffles and oak apples (from their host plant) whet diners' appetites for the gourmet truffle menu at the Ferme St Michel Restaurant in Haute Provence.

one in your pocket in a crowded place, you have only yourself to blame. Franco Taruschio, Wales' distinguished restauranteur, told me that once, while carrying a modest kilo or so of Piedmont truffles from Italy to London, he and his wife were asked to remove themselves and their baggage from the departure lounge at the airport and wait outside until called — even though the fungi were well-insulated in boxes and bags.

The truffle is undoubtedly an acquired taste. Some find it easy, others struggle, but few would admit defeat. There are even some who say they had to force themselves to like it — owning up to what might be taken as a lack of sophistication in much the same spirit as one might admit to the discovery that a light-of-love has unacceptable bedroom habits. While other foodstuffs are a matter of taste, failing to enjoy truffles is not really a choice. "I had to learn to like it, so I do." Those who dislike it the most describe its fragrance in terms which, though scarcely appetising, tell something of the truth: old socks, the locker-room after a rugby match, unwashed underpants, methylated spirits, gas-pump on a wet Saturday — you get the picture.

There has to be a secret. Even detractors would have to admit that tubers *melanosporum* and *magnatum* — more conveniently identified respectively as the Périgord black and the Piedmont white — have a certain allure. But still, no one with half-an-ounce of sense would pay silly prices for a lump of subterranean mushroom that looks and grows like an ill-formed potato, whose texture is unremarkable, and whose taste is — to put it bluntly — not so very different from that of any other fungus.

The secret, I have it on good authority, is in the pheromones. Pheromones, for the uninitiated, are the chemical cocktail produced in the sweat-glands of football fans when they do the Mexican wave, by cabbage white butterflies to warn others where they've laid their eggs, and by people and pigs to attract a mate. They are also, as it happens, produced by truffles as a means of spreading their spores. Not to put too fine a point on it, when ripe and ready, the truffle reeks of sex. You don't get the full impact unless you're there when it's dug. To a truffle-hunter's sow, it says there's a boar about. Dogs, it's usually assumed, have to be taught to look for it and need rewarding in some other way — though some, I have observed, enjoy it too. There are

At the Domaine de Bramerel in Provence, Madame Ayme, the proprietor's wife, dons gloves for the careful work of prising a truffle from its bed — courtesy of her truffle hounds.

other more admissible fragrances present — wet woods, garlic, violets, parmesan, vanilla, chocolate — but it's the pheromones that count.

So is that really the attraction?

"Of course it is," says the chief agrobotanist at the Centre for Trufficulture at Sant'Angelo. "When the women come here to work, we warn them they're taking a risk. It's a joke, naturally. But at the end of a day, we open the windows and go for a walk before we go home to our wives."

Under the botanist's microscope — the instrument on which accurate identification of species depends — are the lacy roots of a baby oak. The leaves, tipped with little prickles, are of a singing green. A trayful of infant trees packed in black plastic, miniature trunks buried in lumpy white gravel, awaits attention nearby. In magnification, the glistening roots, dusted with whitish cobwebs, are tipped with tiny toffee-coloured lollipops. The little globules seem to be giving out a soupy fragrance: heavy, musky, thrilling. I observe that the chief botanist — bearded, fortyish, handsome in a rugged kind of way — has a lovely smile. See? It works.

"Magic, isn't it?"

Indeed it is. Botanically, the truffle is a fruiting body that develops on a mycelium, the fine web of filaments that bonds itself to the roots of certain trees and forms in the process small nodules, transmission points known as mycorrhiza. Truffles are host-specific and the relationship is symbiotic — both parties benefit, though this in the long run suits the guest better than the host. While lesser European species go for beech and fir, the Périgord black (*Tuber melanosporum*), prefers oak and lime, while poplar and hazel appeal to the Piedmont white (*T. magnatum*). While the former likes air and light, and forms its own "burnt" patch under its host, the second needs semi-shade and the presence of bushes to provide a shady understorey. Both need chalky soil, marginal land, the right degree of rainfall, and peace and quiet, to breed, though the white is ecologically pickier than the black and takes longer to come to maturity and fruit. Of these two big hitters of the truffle trade, only the Périgord black is in successful cultivation: there are vast plantations in Spain, and more modest ones in New Zealand, Australia and the USA. But this year, and the reason for my visit, there was news that, after half a century of scientific exploration, poplar trees treated with *T. magnatum* mycorrhiza were coming into fruit.

"We've already had three phone calls out of a possible hundred experimental plantations. That's 3 per cent after twenty years. The black is now 75 per cent after seven years. But it's a start."

It's also money. While the traditional gatherers are the rural poor, the consumers have always been the urban rich. This is only natural, say the middlemen slyly, since the idle rich have always had more need of aphrodisiacs than the working poor. Which may explain why, in the fashionable restaurants of Rome and Milan, a plateful of mama's home-rolled fettucine topped with gossamer ribbons of the right stuff (*Tuber magnatum* 'Pico', the Piedmont white, since you ask, as identified by a botanist called Pico), can set you back 100 euros. Or indeed why, in October 2004, at the beginning of what promised to be a good season, in the truffle market in Sant'Agata Feltria, small pyramids of what look like dusty ivory stones were selling at 3,500 euros a kilo. Meanwhile, in a busy truckers' cafe on what was

*The delicate Piedmont white (*Tuber magnatum*), the truffles of choice in Northern Italy, nestle in a clean white cloth at a market in Alba, one of the major truffle markets in the region.*

once the Appian way, imports from Croatia were on sale, by weight, at around 20 euros a nugget: buy your own and grate it straight onto the pasta.

Of the two high-value truffles, the Piedmont white, which fetches three times the price of the Périgord black, is in season from October till the end of December. The black comes into the market at Christmas, in time for the foie-gras goose, though it's at its best in February and March. They look very different in the hand. The *peridium* – the outer casing – of the Périgord black (*T. melanosporum*) is warty, roughish and ebony-black to deep chestnut; the *glebum* – interior – is brown to dark chocolate colour, patterned with creamy veins; the shape is globular, uneven, with cracks into which dirt can be rubbed by unscrupulous salesmen. The Piedmont white (*T. magnatum*) on the other hand has a smooth, dun-coloured *peridium* and an ivory to greenish *glebum* patterned with pearl. Depending on pressure exerted by the soil, it can be oval, round, or wedge-shaped, like flattened pebbles smoothed by surf.

Both species are absurdly expensive and found in tiny quantities in the wild – and then only in places accessible to a small number of secretive people who mistrust strangers, keep dogs of uncertain temper and carry a pistol in the pocket, just in case. To understand the attraction, you need to eat your truffle fresh, preferably in situ – at least no more that a couple of days from its bed

— though it'll stay good for a week or two wrapped in a scrap of clean linen in the fridge in the salad compartment. The tinned stuff — the little black flecks in the pâté, even aromatized oils — just don't cut the mustard, experience wise. They're fine as a reminder, but that's as far as it goes.

Among lesser varieties, the black summer truffle (*Tuber aestivum*), known in Italy as *scorzone*, is prized for its velvety chestnut-coloured flesh (whose texture is crumbly, releasing tiny bursts of fragrance when grated) and its satisifyingly visible deep ebony skin. The only truffle of gastronomic interest found in Britain — harvested in 2004 and 2005 in considerable quantity in Wiltshire (I was there — it was terrific), the summer truffle is by far the most widespread of Europe's edible subterranean fungi. It is the closest in looks to the Périgord black and shares something of the sublime fragrance of the Piedmont white, for which it's often used as a background flavour, delivering texture as well as fragrance.

The desert truffle (*Terfezia* sp.) is another matter. Traditionally treated in its land of origin as a vegetable, it has a light fragrance, a subtle nutty flavour and a more fibrous texture than the "true" truffle, requiring the application of heat and a generous hand with the spice-jar. Of recent years, imports of an inferior impostor, the Chinese black (*Tuber sinensis*, but also known as *T. indicum* and *T. himalayensis*, though classification is still under debate), caused uproar among the French. And in Italy, there are sinister rumours of a similar impostor, an Oriental white.

Since host-plants are species-specific, it's no good looking under beech trees unless what you hope to find is the summer truffle. No point in searching under poplar unless you anticipate finding the Piedmont white. But anyone looking for the Périgord black among prickly leaved scrub-oaks is on the right track. In the East, the brave soul searching among pine trees under snow in the mountains of Szechuan can expect to be rewarded with the Chinese black (*T. sinensis*) — for what it's worth, which is not much, say the traders.

If you buy your truffle from the official seller in a market, you'll be expected to choose by eye and pay whatever the label says, though the seller may well offer you a sniff. But when buying your truffle directly from the finder — through, say, in France from a rendezvous with a *truffier* in the Périgord or from a furtive bag-carrier under the plane trees at Richerenches in Provence or in Italy from one of the suspicious-looking characters lurking round the Alba market — it's perfectly proper to handle the merchandise before you buy.

Not to do so shows ignorance, increasing your chances of being taken for a ride. And there are a great many ways in which the unscrupulous dealer can get the better of the unwary purchaser. The weight of the truffle can be increased by rubbing mud into a crack in the truffle, lead-shot can be popped into worm-holes or, less seriously, a truffle inadvertently split by a pick or bitten in half by the truffle-hunter's dog, can be held together with a carefully camouflaged toothpick. None of this, however is nearly as likely as being overwhelmed by the seller's banter, his delight in showing you his wares, his sleight of hand when weighing out your choice. And when the difference in cost between one truffle and another is as much as dinner for one at a Michelin-starred restaurant, it's worth paying attention.

USING YOUR NOSE

"To select your truffle, first fondle the goods," says Olga Urbani, who, as Italy's truffle-queen controlling, through the family business, 65 per cent of the world's trade in all truffles, is well qualified to advise. "First the truffle must feel firm, not spongy. Next, appreciate the fragrance – its presence will tell you if the truffle is ripe. If it's immature, there's no fragrance. And if it's too mature, when you lift it to your nose, it'll be disgusting, like petrol, and spongy in the hand, and you'll have to throw it out."

In other words, the nose has it. The olfactory nerves are the least understood of all the equipment that provides us with our five senses – hearing, taste, touch, sight and smell. If the truffle's survival depends on its ability to attract attention by releasing an aroma that speaks directly to the reproductive urges of a passing mammal, it appears that we – apparently the cleverest mammals on the planet – are the last to know about it. Unable to perceive the aroma for ourselves unless it's right under our noses, we're obliged to recruit other creatures – pigs, dogs, even (in one hearsay case in Sussex) a pet badger – to do it for us. We can assume there was a point in our evolutionary arc when noses were as efficient at transmitting information as ears and eyes, and touch.

The truffle exudes one of the most powerful olfactory stimuli any of us will ever encounter. Love it or hate it, once experienced, you'll know it again. Smell, it's generally agreed, is the most primitive of the senses. Considering ourselves civilized, we mistrust the primitive. Given half a chance, we get rid of nose-information altogether, spending vast sums on perfumes and deodorants to make our surroundings smell of something they are not.

The loss of our olfactory warning-system makes sense in evolutionary terms only if the information conveyed is of no further use, or if it has been replaced with a more efficient detection device – a dog, say, or a some other mammalian companion who'll provide the know-how. It's possible, say behaviourists, that nature, taking account of our ability to tame the wild – domesticating the wolf, keeping cows for milk and sheep for meat and wool, even cats to kill rats – simply decided we should carry on the good work and pay the price of our cleverness by becoming dependent on creatures other than ourselves. Or did we just believe we'd lost the ability to use our noses? Was the sense of smell there all along, subtly subversive, playing games with who we think we are?

The truffle is a special case – a foodstuff whose appeal is entirely to the nose, whose fragrance is recognized but never consciously acknowledged for what it is. And yet, if challenged, we probably know exactly what it is. Why, for instance, do the Italians rate the white Piedmont truffle (*Tuber magnatum*) higher than all others, while the French, largely indifferent to the charms of the white even though it's found in their territory, celebrate the black truffle of Périgord (*T. melanospermum*) above all else? Never mind that the Périgord black (as well as *T. aestivum*, the summer-ripening truffle) is found in respectable quantities throughout Italy's truffle-producing provinces, its place in the Italian kitchen is inferior. And there are no recipes in the French culinary canon for the Piedmont white.

I can only begin to explain this intense regional rivalry – it's not merely a matter of who eats garlic – through the development of a sense of smell. My own experience as a mother demonstrated it to me, to some extent. During my family's childhood years, I became aware that sharing a meal is the easiest way of uniting a quarrelsome bunch – four, in my case – a boy and three girls, and all very competitive. Differences, I observed, were easier to settle when food is not only good but shared. Among all societies, however primitive, no quarrelling at table is the first rule of all those who dip into the same dish. And if the sharing

The nose has it. The proprietor of the Domaine de Bramerel, M. Ayme, an expert in the truffle business, knows a good truffle when he smells one.

of a meal conveys a sense of belonging, how, on a practical level, is this created? It must, I reasoned, have something to do with the sense of smell.

The trouble with my theory — that herd-animals such as ourselves needed to smell right to each other in order to work together — was that humans, unlike every other creature dependent on hunting or being hunted, seemed unable to recognize scents unless they were right under their noses. The general view, it seemed, was that any sophisticated olfactory equipment, if we had ever had it at all, had atrophied and vanished around the time we decided two legs were better than four — until, that is, about fifteen years ago, when a paper published in *Nature* magazine revealed the opposite. The paper was brought to my attention by Dr. Miriam Rothschild, the distinguished entymologist for whom I was working as a botanical illustrator on a book on gardening for the benefit of butteflies. She pushed a handful of photocopied pages into my hand. "Well, my dear, you were right. They've found them and they're there. Read that."

Although Dr. Rothschild's reputation rested on her work on fleas — painstaking study which led, ultimately, to the redefining of species according to their host-specific parasites — she remained an enthusiastic generalist. Her methods of working were closer to those of her uncle, Walter Rothschild, the great collector of Tring, than to the bloodless science practised in the lab. When she wanted to know how butterflies behave, she simply took a camping-stool into her garden at dawn and remained there until dusk. This had led her to conclude that the butterflies have a perfectly well-developed sense of smell, used, among other things, to select the leaves suitable for caterpillars. Earlier in the day, we had been discussing scent-marking by cabbage whites as a means of communicating to other butterflies to beware the leaves on which they had already laid eggs. She found the notion of communication by scent entirely plausible, though she had always pointed out its non-existence in humans. "Which doesn't mean it's not there. Just that we haven't found it yet."

The article in question delivered the information that a little pair of receptors, nairs, at the back of the throat, were not atrophied at all, but fully functional, transfering sophisticated olfactory information directly into the brain in a way which exactly mirrored the sensory devices of our fellow mammals, danger-signals and all.

The truth is we have no trouble recognizing the scents we like or dislike, even if we can't say exactly why. This, it appears, is because smell simply bypasses the usual intellectual channels and goes straight to the primitive part of the brain that has control of speech and gives rise to the feelings we call animal instinct.

As a recipe-writer, I know well enough how hard it is to describe a flavour to someone who's never experienced it. Wine-experts have developed a sophisticated vocabulary to define a great wine or even a bad one – but how and why one wine resonates on the palate and another doesn't remains a mystery. Sight and sound have very precise terms of description – they can be recorded and reproduced. But flavour cannot be stored between hard covers or captured on recording machinery, or hung on the wall. Useless to try to define it in any other way than by referring to comparable tastes and scents – it just is what it is.

So if the stuff that makes the truffle memorable has to do with the presence of pheromones – a chemical cocktail defined by the dictionary as a substance produced and released into the environment by an animal or insect, affecting the behaviour of others of its species, and if pheromones primarily appeal to the reproductive urge – the one which keeps the bloodline in business – it stands to reason that a noseful of the right stuff calls up an instinct we share with every other living creature on the planet. And if, by some alchemy, pheromones allow us to make the difference between ourselves and other species with which we cannot reproduce, why should they not, when added to a cocktail of aromas that they somehow heighten and mark as memorable, allow us to identify the scent of those with whom we may procreate? Thus leading to the creation of – well – romance and poetry and the songs of the troubadours, the kind of stuff that encourages people to mate for life.

All this might go some way towards explaining why the truffle produces a substance so deliriously attractive that any creature which recognizes it had no choice but to search it out, dig it up and gobble it down. And since the ripening season is very short and the area of production very limited, the truffle has to ensure that once eaten it's never forgotten. As a strategy, it can't be bettered.

If certain foodstuffs are more memorable than others – the ones which command high prices in the marketplace such as caviar, chocolate, vanilla and, of course, the truffle – there's reason to believe that foods endowed with pheromones are the most memorable of all.

The chemists, bless them, have come up with an explanation – several, as it happens – that identifies the complex process by which we select what we like to eat. The main function of taste, they say, is to warn the stomach of what's on the way. Like smell, the chemists say, the sense of taste seems to be more of a danger-warning device than a pleasure-giver. Receptors for taste are found on the tongue and around other parts of the mouth. These – around 6,000 taste-buds, if you're counting – respond to foods mixed in saliva on the tongue. Since the cells on the tongue divide, renewing themselves completely every few days, the receptors you have today will not be the ones you use next week. Bang go the memory-buds. To survive, the information must be stowed away elsewhere: in the brain. The problem here is that the brain – or that part of it that governs the intellect – does not seem particularly well-adapted to delivering food-memories in anything but the vaguest terms.

Mirabel Osler in *The Elusive Truffle*, a memorable chronicle of gastronomic travels among the French, puts her finger on the problem: "Among gustatory experiences sought by gourmets, few can match up to the truffle. There are others – your first taste of caviar, the moment you realize the scent in your nostrils is durian – which are memorable, but none has the same effect on the emotions. While other foodstuffs can be a solitary experience, everyone can remember with whom they shared the first truffle. . . the memory of the occasion is branded on my culinary skin even if I can no longer conjure up the taste any more than I can recall the scent."

This elusive concept – the ability to remember a taste without being able to describe it – is explored by Dr. Neil Martin of Middlesex University. There is one region of the brain, explains Dr. Martin, that picks up the sensory properties of food, and a separate region that relates to its emotional quality – whether we like what's in our mouths or not. All areas of olfactory and gustatory reception – nose, receptors in the tongue, mouth and throat – pass the information on to different parts of the brain. Among these, are the hippocampus, a structure that deals with memory formation, and the amygdala, a small conglomerate that appears to monitor the environment for danger. The result is a powerhouseful of information, all dropped neatly into the filing cabinet without so much as a label, bypassing the intellect altogether, ready to pop up when given the nudge. Flavour is a combination of taste and smell. And smell, though commonly considered the least important of the five senses, is actually repsonsible for 80per cent of flavour. And if smell is the truffle's strongest card, small wonder it sticks in the mind.

And as if that were not enough, the process used to identify taste – salt, sweet, sour, bitter – is also used to pick up *umami*, a substance whose virtues are uncannily like those of the truffle. Umami, the controversial fifth taste, was identifed a century ago in Japan as present in meat, certain fish, cheese, tomatoes, human breast milk and fungi. It is most obvious in the form of monosodium glutamate (MSG) – the taste-powder used in Chinese cooking for enhancing the flavour of other tastes, an effect achieved by sharpening the appetite. And the truffle, it's widely acknowledged, enhances flavour and sharpens appetite.

THE GASTRONOMIC MEASURE OF THE TRUFFLE

Paul Levy, gastronomic adventurer and passionate gourmet, has no doubt of the truffle's effect on the jaded palate. "Of course it's an appetite-sharpener; the best there is. I remember when we – my wife, Penny, and I – had been on a gastronomic blowout and we were booked into one of the great restaurants of Lyons. When we got there, we were incapable of swallowing another bite. When the chef came through to greet us, we explained we couldn't eat. He smiled and said he understood. Then he sat us at the bar and brought us a glass of champagne, a truffle, a knife and a salt-shaker, and then he left us alone. Twenty minutes later, we were ready to dine."

If the truffle's most remarkable property is its ability to gild the lily – and any lily, from lobster to eggs or potatoes to steak – why not ice-cream or crème caramel, or even truffle-flavoured chocolate truffles? These last might seem like over-egging the pudding, but they are the latest must-haves on the menu in *La Truffe Noire*, which, as far as I am aware, is the world's only restaurant devoted entirely to the subterranean fungus, and placed, most appropriately, in Brussels, home of the European Union's plumpest expense accounts, and the only city (with the possible exception of Las Vegas) where the money available can match the prices. Its chef-proprietor, Luigi Ciciriello – a native of Puglia and surprisingly for an Italian, a passionate devotee of the Périgord black – has earned a Michelin star and one of the highest ratings in the Gault Millau.

A measure of its success is the opening of a cooked-food shop and an affordable brasserie a few streets down. The idea of paying the place a visit in truffle-season was irresistible. On my way to the Périgord from the Channel ports, I made the detour for curiosity's sake. On a blustery day in mid-December, the *Atelier de la Truffe*, the brasserie side of the business, had slowed down for the afternoon break. At around the time when English ladies of a certain age take tea, the place, apart from a couple of rain-drenched shoppers sipping coffee, was deserted. I realized that the hour was inconvenient, but nevertheless, this was an all-day brasserie and there might be something I could taste.

The young man behind the counter left his glass polishing to enquire after my requirements. With the Piedmont white at the end of the season and the Périgord black not yet in full swing and, considering the time of day, my gastronomic expectations were not high. No problem, said the young man. The full menu – truffle-showered pastas, risottos and other hot dishes which changed on a daily basis – was not, he explained apologetically, available until the chef returned for the evening session. However, he could, if I wished, prepare a plate of their veal *carpaccio* with truffles, one of Signor Ciciriello's dishes and something he could easily prepare for a weary traveller such as myself.

I accepted with enthusiasm. The young man busied himself behind the bar. Rosy slices of meat cut across the grain, lean and semi-transparent, were laid in a single layer on a large white plate. The arrangement was finished with a sprinkle of finely slivered green-leaf celery, a turn of the pepper mill and a trickle of olive oil. Perfect.

Now for the important question. Was the finishing to be white or black? Perhaps I would like a little help with the decision. The young man smiled, bent down, straightened up, placed two glass jars on the counter and removed their stoppers.

The scent eddied around the room, first one and then the other. The chance to compare the one with the other is rare. The window in time in which both are available fresh, in full ripeness, is too narrow – a matter of days or a week or two at most. Experienced like this, in quick succession, the two fragrances are as different as – how to explain it in non-gustatory terms? – jasmine and rose, platinum and gold. The olfactory equivalent of contralto and soprano. Neither preferable to the other. And yet, perhaps the black for its gutsy earthiness, or, then again, the white for its airy delicacy.

Like a diamond dealer offering a pair of royal gems, the young man picked his treasure from their snowy papers, first one and then the other, and held them out. One, a glittering sphere of rough-chipped ebony, the other smooth as an egg, an ivory pebble. What's to be done? When handed the golden apple, Paris chose Aphrodite over wise Athena and mighty Hero – and landed himself with Helen and trouble for Troy. Looks will out. The surface of the rosy calf-flesh was showered with creamy ribbons. I chose the white, inhaled the fragrance – and, like an addict offered the drug of choice, felt my heartbeat quicken.

Hand me a truffle, or parts thereof, and my heart begins to race. I've no idea why this should be so, or if it's a reaction common to all who share my passion. Or if, and I wouldn't bet against it, it's just a matter of chemistry.

If pheromones are the subtext, other more admissible fragrances (quince, chocolate, violets, honey, musk) make the truffle valuable to the cook. As with other fungi, the flavours work best in association with olive oil, goose-fat, soft cheese, butter and cream. That is to say, with something smooth, unctuous and soothing to the taste-buds. At the Oxford Symposium in 2004 (subject: Wild Food) someone brought a jar of truffles grated into *lardo*, a very white, very delicate, herb-cured pig-fat. The entire conference – academics, recipe writers, TV chefs and all – was very excited about it and talked about it for the rest of the weekend. This I know because I arrived too late to taste it and was unable to get a handle on the fuss.

HOW TO EAT IT?

When considering suitable recipes, it's as well to take account of discernible difference in fragrance. It's *personal,* of course, but I'd put it like this: if the Piedmont white is a very attentive husband, the Périgord black is a bit of the rough. As for the others, consider them mere flirtation – fun while it lasts, as long as you don't get caught.

Of the two principles, the flesh of the Piedmont white is elastic, silky-smooth and delicate. It should never be cooked. After a gentle brushing under running water, it may be shaved into transparent ribbons – preferably with a purpose-made instrument, though a potato-slicer will do – and dropped directly onto a heap of steaming pasta – polenta, fonduta, risotto – when the warmth will release the scent.

The Périgord black can also be eaten raw: most memorably, to my mind, for breakfast – cut into thick matchsticks and dipped in a soft-boiled egg, in whose company it has spent the previous night. Just the same, its firm, slightly crumbly flesh and robust fragrance can withstand the application of prolonged heat in a casserole or being simmered in a slow-cooked broth.

If traditional recipes call for different treatment for the white and the black truffle, modern chefs take the view that neither species should be cooked at all. This principle, when applied to by-products of the trade, such as truffle pastes and fragranced oils, allows simple foods such as pasta to be given complex flavours in a fraction of the time it would take to produce a traditional recipe – say a *sauce Périgourdine* based on the black truffle, or a melted-cheese *fonduta* finished with shavings of the white.

Paul Levy has no doubts of the rightness of the raw brigade: "I don't think truffles of any kind should ever be cooked at all. They lose their fragrance. The best way to eat them is raw, cut in fine slivers with a knife, with salt and butter. You can do it like American oreo cookies, two slices sandwiched together with unsalted butter with the top sprinkled with salt-crystals. One very famous London chef did it for a group of us with a slice of white and a slice of black – very pretty, like black and white chocolate – and then he couldn't resist, and he cooked the things, and that was the end of that."

There's a school of thought that maintains that for a dish to be considered traditional and therefore somehow more valuable than others, there must be a myth attached. And the truffle is well-endowed with myth.

Eggs and truffles are a winning combination, garnished here with oak leaves and acorns – a reminder of the black truffle's natural habitat.

Truffles – from Legend to Science

The truffle owes its fame as much to the poet as the cook. Myth, the process by which our ancestors explained the inexplicable, combined with reality to produce — well — a reputation. Which is just as well for the truffle's prospects as a foodstuff, since it's hard to find, unreliable in cropping, almost impossible to cultivate, and delivers scarcely enough nourishment to satisfy a dormouse.

In fact, if it wasn't for reputation, well, no-one would have wanted it all. And if its reputation is indeed its fortune, how was it earned? Scarcity plays a part, as does chemistry. Food-historian Maguelonne Toussaint-Samat describes its allure: "Adding the attraction of mystery to its magical fragrance and supposedly aphrodisiac qualities . . . prudently, nature has made it very rare." In the hands of a cook of reasonable proficiency, it raises the ordinary to the sublime. And one whiff of its intense perfume, say the poets, delivers everything achieved by rhyming moon with June — and more.

The first truffle, the legend goes among the French (always ready to claim priority in matters culinary), was found in the woods of the Périgord by an old sow which, though she had given birth to many piglets in her time, had outlived her usefulness. Her days being numbered, the swineherd allowed her an outing to the woods to gorge herself one last time on acorns. Rooting in the soil, she dug up something black and pungent. The swineherd, fearing poison, tried to snatch it from her jaws. Skipping from his grasp, she chewed and swallowed. Suitors suddenly appeared from all sides and fell into an amatory frenzy, leading, as is the way with pigs, to many unions, which led in turn to many comely piglets, plump as plums. Thereafter every autumn the

A 19th-century French print of a truffler with his pig. In modern times, pigs are very rarely used as foragers since they're hard to separate from their finds.

sow was led to the woods where, regular as clockwork, she found her fungi and called her suitors, and every spring came yet more piglets to swell the household coffers when market day came round.

Meanwhile the swineherd, whose own union had never been blessed with issue, searched out and ate the magic fungus for himself, then found another and gave it to his wife. Results were as anticipated. Thereafter, every year, his wife gave birth to bouncing baby boys, thirteen in all — more than enough to attract the interest of the lord who owned the forest. The landlord told the king and. . . well, the rest is history.

ANCIENT RELICS

Archaeologists, rooting around in Stone Age middens, have found the debris of several species of truffle in quantities and places unexplained by nature. Those who searched the winter woods for food were undoubtedly far more sensitive than us to the subtleties of earth and air: the sweet breath of berries ripe on the branch, the dry fragrance of nut-meat swollen in the shell, the particular fragrance emitted by leaves or stalks or flowers bruised in passing.

Picture us, if you will, among our human ancestors — tool-using, god-fearing, ourselves in every sense — and that we are walking through woods in truffle territory in the depths of winter. The sun has risen. The earth is cold at dawn, but not frozen as it is at night, when it's hard and unyielding to the unshod foot. Sunlight slants through the branches of tall trees. Underfoot, last year's leaves are tipped with frost. We move swiftly, setting our feet down with care, wary of alerting predators. Our feet, being naked, allow us to read the contours of the earth, understanding through the thick cushions of sole and heel, the paper-thin skin of the instep and the soft pads of the toes all we need to know of what lies beneath. As we move through the trees, we are aware not only of the noises made by other creatures who share our woods, but of the sounds we make ourselves as the terrain changes — wetness of moss, dryness of twigs — warning our companions, travelling behind in single file, of hazards just ahead. We can trust, too, that our companions, pack-animals like ourselves, will pick up the scent our bodies exude when frightened or aroused, or even, it can be supposed, other more subtle emotional changes communicated without the need for speech.

Our ancestors – descendants of those few who, around 100,000 years ago, left the shelter of their African beginnings – took shelter in the caves that pit the limestone cliffs of Europe's mighty rivers. We have evidence of the working of their minds, since they spent the long evenings of the winter months tracing images of the creatures they hoped to kill when the sun returned. In the cold months, reluctant to move far from shelter, they ate what came to hand, though in winter there was little to gather and still less to hunt. Their prey-animals – cattle, horses, deer – had moved in great migratory herds as soon as the days shortened to the warmer lands of the south.

Only the predators were left: bears, wolves, creatures adapted to a cycle of winter hibernation that our ancestors, not long out of their African homeland, had not had time to acquire. Hibernation is to be recommended in a cold climate – there's no need to eat; our ancestors, however, needed to feed. Since meat from prey-animals – small rodents and reptiles excepted – was unobtainable in winter, foodstuffs were limited to gatherings: roots, berries, nuts – and fungi. These last, the coprophages – eaters of dead things – had to be approached with caution, since while some were edible and good, others were known to be poisonous. A few, the shamam's mushrooms, brought visions – multi-coloured dreams – though these, if used in ignorance, brought death. Most powerful of these, the scarlet toadstool, was worshipped as a god and used in time of war to stimulate the urge to kill. Others, more benevolent, worked magic in other ways, stirring the heart and heating the blood – and among these, if reputation serves it right, is the truffle. How opportune, how perfectly appropriate, that a subterranean fungus capable of withstanding frost, whose main attraction is a chemical compound that exactly mimics the scent of procreation, should come to maturity at a time when it's needed most. For those for whom the sun was the source of all life, midwinter is the time to take a mate and by setting an example, renew the earth's fecundity and spread her seeds.

Later in our history, when the unruly feasts of pagan times gave way to the church-led festival with which Christians mark the birth of Christ, a few of the old habits, outlawed by the early Fathers, slipped back into Christmas feast. Holly and mistletoe are the most obvious of these, though there are plenty of others: blazing fires and the need for candlelight as well as the rowdy drunkeness with which we celebrate the change of year, while the hallucinogenic toadstool – scarlet-capped and blotched with snowy white –

hides in the uniform of Santa Claus. The truffle, too, has made its way over the centuries to pop up in its land of origin at Provence's *souper maigre* — the sobre fasting supper of Christmas Eve — where it is dropped in ink-black slivers on the ivory surface of a salt-cod cream. It reappears again a few hours later at the celebration feast following midnight Mass, layered into the rosy liver of a fattened goose or slipped beneath the breast of a roasted partridge.

CLASSICAL TRUFFLES

The truffle, culinary historians suggest, first appeared on the record with the ancient Greeks, sybarites and admirers of the good things of the flesh. In the days when Socrates philosophized with Plato, a dish of *udnon* was served to the elders by a would-be citizen of Athens. (However, since Libya is quoted as the source and *udnon* — subterranean foodstuff — is a description applied to anything that forms bumps in the soil, the dish was most likely composed of a related species to the European truffle, desert truffles of the *Terfezia* tribe which thrives in sandy soil.) Be that as it may, both species clearly spoke the same language. Aristotle declared it aphrodisiacal. Pythagoras agreed.

While its fragrance is undoubtedly its fortune, the sybaritic Greeks valued it for other reasons. Its conception — the manner in which it suddenly appeared, its lack throughout its lifetime of visible means of support — appealed to a society that favoured the notion of unreliable gods, infantile and wilful, who made things happen. Whenever wars were lost or love went unrequited, or something in nature could not be explained in any other way, Immortals took the blame. Truffles, whose sudden appearance was unexplained in any other way, were thought to be seedlings of the gods, warts on the earth's skin, the infant sons of sorcerers, offspring of witches.

To Roman epicures, the truffle was simply earth-fruit, *Tuber terrae*, though, since the term can equally be applied to any root or bulb, no-one can be certain which species is meant (either by the Romans or the Greeks), though historians suggest these were still *Terfezia* rather than the European truffle of the family *Tuber*, the "true" truffles prized by modern cooks. Apicius rinses his truffles in wine, dusts them with pepper and roasts them in hot embers — a recipe to raise the body's heat and improve performance in the bedroom. On Lesbos, romantic Sappho's isle, the truffles of Mytelene were admired, though whether this was for the enhancement of sapphic dalliance is not revealed.

Plutarch, observing when and where the truffle was formed, agreed in principle that the truffle was not, as with all other fungi, born of earth, but formed by fusion, appearing at the exact point where a clap of thunder met a bolt of lightning. Theophrastus, Aristotle's pupil, had no doubt that he was right. "For *udnon* to be formed," he says, "There must be lightning allied with thunder. And if there be neither," he adds, with admirable brevity, "There will be none." The truffle could never be cultivated, observed Nicander of Cleos, poet-gardener at the time of Christ: while other mushrooms might be encouraged to sprout on compost placed between the roots of fig trees, the method did not work with truffles which, being the product of the internal heat of the earth, could not persuaded to fruit unless they so chose.

Cheating started early in the story. The naturalist Pliny, who met his end peering into the erupting heart of Mount Vesuvius as its lava drowned Pompeii, reported on black deeds in the truffle trade in the city of Cartagena: the Minister of Justice, charged with punishing dishonesty in the market place, it seemed, had cracked his teeth on a denarius (a coin), embedded in a truffle as a makeweight to increase the value. To add to the confusion, the naturalist added that the fungus family known as *Tuber terrae* might be black, red or white, but never larger than a quince, an allusion unlikely to be lost on his audience, since everyone knew the quince — Eve's true apple — was the fruit eaten at weddings to ensure the bride's fertility.

Rome could never get enough of the truffle. Lucullus, Rome's most lavish banquet-thrower, served truffles to his guests when, sated by too much flamingo-tongue and peacock-brain, they couldn't eat another morsel. Marcus Aurelius ate truffles, on his physician's advice, to improve his performance in the bedroom — too much, however, the medical man advised, would bring on melancholia. Apicius provides the first practical recipes, recommending spit-roasting and sauces in the Arab style — but it's to be supposed that the truffles he had in mind are the desert varieties, though they might equally well have been other fungi: maybe the mop-topped morel or even the gold-capped Caesar's mushroom, *Amanita caesarea*, whose toxic lookalike was fed by Empress Agrippina to her husband Claudius in sufficient quantity to kill.

Satirists — scourge of politicians then as now — found the truffle a useful metaphor for decadence. The playwright Juvenal, looking for a way to tell his audience a character was worthless, had only to feed him a dish of truffles.

THE TRUFFLE IN EUROPEAN HISTORY

It would be impossible to know the exact moment when the "true" truffle of modern times replaced the desert truffle, *Terfezia*, appreciated in Classical times, on the tables of Italy and France. However, during the fourteenth century, an exuberant truffle hunt with pigs and peasants is depicted with impeccable detail in the exquisite Book of Hours, a visual calendar of life in rural medieval France commissioned by the Duc de Berry. So fond was the duke of his woodland crop, and so confident of its efficacy as an aphrodisiac, that he supplied large quantities of his ink-black treasure for consumption by the royal couple at the nuptial banquet marking the union of Charles the Fair with Isabeau of Bavaria, thus informing all capable of reading the signs that every effort had been made to deliver the desired result – a child of unquestioned parentage to rule both roosts.

Throughout the Middle Ages, a time when Mother Church was at her most powerful, the truffle disappeared altogether from the rich man's menu (no-one records the daily dinner of the poor). Though, since the king's forest continued to be cropped by hump-backed pigs of the old breed under the care of swineherds, it is unlikely that the poor did not continue to search for it and trade in it, at least in secrecy. In the age of superstition, when medical men were magicians – sorcerers, soothsayers, weavers of spells – the truffle found itself new admirers among practitioners of the black arts, who found its attributes irresistible. A substance of undeniable mystery, subterranean, either black as night or bone-white, drawing sustenance from the dead, could only be powerful magic. For those whose chemical armoury consisted of "eye-of-newt and heart-of-toad", the truffle, with its strange perfume and even stranger lifestyle, spoke of the triumph of life over death. The Church, reserving resurrection for God alone, was outraged. The stuff was declared doubly dangerous, since the perfume for which it was valued was held to induce the kind of behaviour among celibate priests and nuns that could lead to the birth of children, which might in turn, God forbid, lead to disputes over the church's property, never mind the havoc caused among their flocks. Sermons were preached against it from the pulpit. The truffle was no longer the cook's darling, but the work of the devil.

The truffle returned to favour during the Renaissance, as the power of the Church diminished and art and literature returned to their classical roots. Somewhat poignantly, it was the Vatican's librarian, Platina, a powerful advocate during the fifteenth century of Roman culinary arts, who spoke warmly of truffles in *De honesta voluptate* (Of permissible pleasures) and completed the rehabilitation. As soon as the word was out, every royal banquet had to have its dishes lavishly dressed with truffles. At the Palace of Fontainebleau, the chefs of François I, arch-rival of the Holy Roman Emperor and a man whose appetite for war was almost as great as his delight in the pleasures of the flesh, included truffles in every course. Foremost among those who admired the truffle for its qualities as an aphrodisiac were the Marquis de Sade (no need to ask why), and the Comtesse du Barry (*belle-lettriste* and wit) — whose rival for the king's affections was Madame de Pompadour — so she may well have had need of it. Rasputin recommended the truffle to the Tsar as a blood thickener and strengthener for the Imperial bloodline — one, as it turned out, sorely in need of strengthening. Emperor Napoléon, triumphant on the battlefield, also ate truffles for strength in a battle he never expected to win — tussles between the covers with his fiery Empress Josephine.

As for Italy, her cooks, once their native truffles had been found and valued, chose and cooked them according to the territory, looking to Piedmont for recipes for the autumn-fruiting white, and to Umbria for dishes for the winter-fruiting black, even though both white and black are found in quantity in other regions. Of the two, *Tuber melanosporum* and *T. magnatum*, the latter is wholeheartedly preferred in Italy to the first, and known as "*magnato*" — the magnate's truffle — proof enough of its value. In *Cuciniera Piemontese*, published in Turin in 1798, recipes are given for baking truffles wrapped in pastry or simmering them gently in oil with parsley, shallots, prosciutto and "*sciampagna*" — no need to define the species once the region is mentioned.

THE HAND OF SCIENCE

Meanwhile, in France, the intellectuals of the Age of Reason, exploring the revolutionary notion that the natural world might continue to function without divine intervention, rejected the Church and threw in their lot with the scientists. Scientific minds, brought to bear on territory previously left to farmers, forced changes in attitude as well as practice, and, over the course of time, alterations in farming methods, facilitated by machinery, fertilizers and pesticides, changed the face of the land for ever. The wealthy landowners' interests were more frivolous, encouraging science to take an interest in growing exotic foodstuffs — among them the truffle. Its requirements were studied under the microscope, ancient authorities consulted on its habit. And while no reasonable person would agree that such a substance could be possibly be formed by a clap of thunder and a flash of lightning, it was undoubtedly true that summer storms promoted the truffle's growth, so biologists conceded a grain of truth in myth. For the first time it seemed that the truffle — as with the cultivated mushroom, offspring of *Agaricus campestris*, already grown in great quantity in limestone caves near Paris — might be induced to crop in territory not of its own choosing.

In more recent times, two world wars have led to the loss of many of those who worked the land, leaving much of the truffle's natural territory uncropped. By the 1950s, the shortage of labour — as a result of two successive generations of young men killed in battle — led to a drift to the towns and to depopulation of the countryside in France and Italy. The result, a situation not yet reversed, was the loss of rural skills acquired over the centuries, including ancient methods of agriculture that brought marginal lands into cultivation, serving the truffle well. And the truffle, its existence threatened by the loss not only of suitable terrain but the disappearance of its chief spore-spreader, had to find a new sponsor.

In the nick of time, science took over. As a crop of proven economic value, the truffle, the scientists agreed, was well worth cultivating. All it needed was the right conditions, and who better to provide them than a new generation of microscope-savvy agrobotanists whose sponsors — multi-national companies in search of new and valuable crops — were prepared to fund their work. With one bound, the truffle was free. Or, at least, set fair to join the great botanical harem of plants valued for mind-appeal, as pleasure-givers and botanical survivalists, at whom humankind is prepared to throw large amounts of money, land and time. Such plants are identified by Dr. Michael Pollen in *The Botany of Desire* as desirable rather than simply useful. Among his selections — the tulip for beauty, the cider-apple for its ability to induce

Truffle under the microscope: an illustration from a 19th-century French natural history book, showing the local flora and fauna, and indeed the local truffle, enlightening us as to what lies beneath its rough exterior.

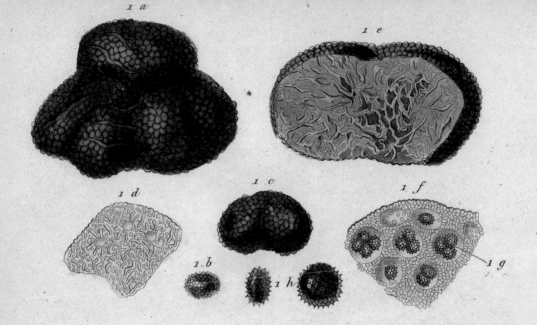

1 a   1 e

1 d   1 c   1 f

1 b   1 h   1 g

2

1. Truffe.   2. Troupiale.

merriment, the marijuana plant for its mind-altering property — each owes its success to a willingness to tailor its evolutionary process to suit its benefactor. Which begs the question, who needs whom?

The truffle is surely a candidate for Dr. Pollen's list. By establishing dependency on its chief propagator, the truffle has everything to gain and nothing to lose from its close association with man. Within fifty years of surrendering its independence — give or take what little remains in the wildwood — the truffle has established itself as, if not actually a world-wide crop, one with a future. And all this without altering its ecological requirements one whit. Not bad for a lump of vegetation in imminent danger of extinction.

So who's the fall-guy now? And while the question's on the table, there's another candidate, an insect, which also has an interest: the truffle-fly, a little reddish insect that lays its eggs in the vicinity of the ripe truffle, and by its presence draws the attention of the predator. Whoever or whatever consumes the truffle passes both truffle-spores and fly-eggs through its digestive system, creating an environment in which the eggs may safely hatch, so this system suits all three: fungus, fly and predator. Unless, that is, the circle is broken and the truffle is deposited somewhere unfriendly to its spores.

Consider, too, the host-trees on which the truffle depends — oak, hazel, poplar, lime, beech — that now find themselves in places in which, in a million years, they would never have reached alone. These, along with the truffle spores attached to their hair-fine roots, transport an entirely alien micro-ecosystem to a region that may alter it for good or bad. It's evolution — change is good. And if we do not change, we die.

CULINARY TABOOS

The link between hardship and certain foodstuffs haunts our history, imposing taboos on where and how particular foods may be consumed, or even if they may be consumed at all. Taboos — prohibitions, religious and secular — evolve for many reasons, practical as well as mystical, many of them serving simply to differentiate one group of people from another.

The desert truffle, though featured by the Greeks and Romans and appreciated in the sophisticated cuisines of Arab lands, is mentioned in neither the Old Testament nor the New, though many other foodstuffs feature. Perhaps this particular prohibition is religious, since fungi have a reputation as trance-inducers, tongue-looseners: dangerous territory for a people whose mission is to follow the word of God. In the lands of the Arabs, though mention is made of truffles in the gastronomy of Al-Andaluz, the settled territories of southern Spain, the text known as *The Baghdad Cookery Book*, one of the earliest records of the Arab kitchen, includes no fungi recipes at all. Perhaps the reasons are practical — the Arabs are a nomadic people, and could therefore never be sure that fungi safely gathered in one terrain will not be of a different nature in another.

Less obvious are those taboos applied to foodstuffs for emotional reasons because they are associated with a time people don't want to remember. Certain foodstuffs, among them the truffle, acquire their prohibitions simply by being in the right place at the wrong time. The process is subtle. While the rich saw the truffle as pleasure acquired for money, and few would have cared or known where and how it was found, its reputation among the poor was darker. For the rural poor, the truffle was a cash-crop exchangeable for money, and, since its shelf-life was short, the quicker the better. In times of peace this was simply a matter of making an arrangement with the middleman — the egg-woman, the silkworm-pedlar, the travelling distiller — who took the goods to market and found a buyer. But in times of want — in the plague-years or when the crop failed, or when soldiers laid waste the fields in time of war — the market vanished altogether and the truffle stayed in the larder of whoever had found it, to be dropped in the beanpot instead of meat, or shaved over the pasta when the cheese-store was empty.

Similar taboos apply to grain foods fed to livestock when times are good but eaten by their masters when times are hard. Such foods, tarred with poverty's brush, become famine food. Among bread-baking peoples, famine foods are oats and barley; among meat-eaters, turnips and roots. When the staple fails, people have no choice but to move down the food chain. To those who survive, famine is a sign of failure, weakness, and a cause for shame. When the potato crop failed in Scotland's Western Isles in the nineteenth century, maize-flour was the foodstuff sent to relieve famine. As a result, a century and a half later, when I lived and cooked in the Hebrides, I found the islanders still wary of polenta, however elegantly dressed. "It reminds us of those days of the blight, when the boats brought in the famine relief," my neighbour informed me — never mind that the memory was a century old.

Since the truffle was eaten by the poor only as a last resort, the stigma remained even when times improved. Too valuable to eat when times were good, it was consigned to the poor man's pot only when it couldn't be turned to account in any other way. In Spain, to those who lived through the terrible years of the Civil War in the 1930s, the truffle remains a substance of doubtful reputation, though several species are found in abundance throughout the land and in areas well-endowed with foraging pigs. This strange situation was brought to my attention when, travelling in truffle-territory in the 1980s in search of regional recipes, I found few willing to admit to knowing it, even though the common name, *criadillas de tierra* — earth testicles — indicated an understanding of what it looked like and where it could be found — not to mention an awareness of its distinctive fragrance.

Although a few were prepared to admit to gathering truffles to sell, no-one would admit to having tasted them. Reasons given were varied. One man — a strong supporter of the old regime — told me they were a parasite unknown in the region until the death of the old dictator, which, to a certain extent, was true, since the vast plantations near Soria were established in the 1980s. And furthermore, added another, they were food for the Moors, sufficient in itself as a reason not to eat them in a Christian country whose patron saint, Santiago de Compostela, is known by the name of *Matamoros*, Moor-slayer. Although, relenting a little, he added that I might find what I sought in Morella, where they did things differently.

Morella, an elegant monastery town to the north of Valencia, where resistance to the old dictator had been fiercest, did indeed do things differently. My enquiries led me to a certain corner of a certain bar at a certain time — its location never to be divulged on pain of death by rotten truffle — where I was to ask for Josep. Josep, though an old man and a little too fond of the brandy, was very knowledgeable. As a matter of fact, I was told in confidence, it was he who was responsible for supplying the truffles to the traders from the Périgord. How could it be, I enquired, that although people seemed to know what the truffles were, and people were willing to gather them and trade them, no-one would admit to eating them? Josep considered my question gravely and shook his head.

This lithograph depicts a 19th-century French truffle hunter, bending to see what his truffle dogs have unearthed.

"You are not from the territory."

"That makes a difference?"

"Of course. The *criadillas* are for those too poor to eat meat. Poverty is shameful. We have pride — *orgullo*. We will tell you we eat chicken when what we eat is rabbit. And if we tell you we know what the *criadillas* taste like, you'll know it's because we were poor. During the war — Franco's war — all of us were poor, all of us were hungry. People starved. But afterwards we did not speak of it. At that time, I was only a boy, my mother sent me into the woods to bring home what the pigs ate. Everyone knows that pigs and people eat the same things. And when I found the *criadillas*, my mother would drop them in the pot so the beans would taste of meat. Later we kept a pig for ourselves, and I would go into the forest and fetch acorns and roots just for him. But if I brought home *criadillas*, my mother would put them in the pot even when there was meat. I knew because the beanpot tasted particularly good. She never told my father and we never spoke of it. No-one did. And then, when the dealers came and told us about the money, people began to change their view. These days there's a truffle restaurant in Morella and they serve what they say are traditional dishes — goose and chicken, and milk-fed lamb, things only rich people ate. You can't blame them for that. No-one would pay good money for a bean-pot, truffled or not."

The diet of despair, remembered in times of plenty, can never again be tasted with pleasure.

VENERATING THE TRUFFLE

The idea of ownership — that what had always been food-for-free might belong to someone other than the finder — is a modern idea. The more the truffle market expanded, the more attractive the gathering became. Inevitably, once it was understood that the right host-trees planted in suitable conditions could be encouraged or induced to become truffle-bearing — farming in its most primitive form on marginal land with steep slopes and stony terrain — the poorest and least desirable part of any landholding — became potentially valuable. And since disputes over truffle territory are particularly hard to resolve since the crop cannot easily be quantified — one year the crop is good, another year there's nothing — accusations of cheating are inevitable. Further complications arise under the Code Napoléon that operates in both France and Italy in which ownership in all property passes equally to all children of a marriage and is usually resolved by one member of the family taking responsibility for farmland and charging siblings for his labour while all retain an interest in what the land produces. On non-arable land — pasture and woodlands deliberately set aside for the hunter — gatherings are traditionally left to chance. Truffles are a different matter: even if all family members agree to share the bounty among themselves, there's sure to be a neighbour down the road who sees it differently, whose forefathers have been cropping these particular patches since — well — since their ancestors first stumbled out of the cave.

Wilful in the wild, the truffle is just as unreliable in captivity. Even when grown on the right trees on dedicated ground by those who understand exactly how it should be treated, it remains a random crop. And just to set the record straight, a plantation truffle, once liberated from its bed, cannot be distinguished from a truffle of spontaneous growth: there's no discernible difference in fragrance or flavour, though some will tell you they can tell it apart in other ways. To those who scour the wildwood, the plantation truffle is of no more interest than a rabbit in a hutch: a tame thing, women's business, lacking the thrill of the chase. Which may, perhaps, explain the enthusiasm with which otherwise honest men steal other people's truffles, risking life and limb (and heavy fines) to clear a rival's woods.

For the successful hunter, the cash, though welcome, is not the sole reward. Among those accustomed to fill their larders, even if partially, by their own labours, money is not something by which a man should be judged. Wine from a well-tended vineyard, oil pressed from a man's own olives, his wife's way with the fruit of the mulberry tree, these are the things whose worth can be measured. And for the truffle-hunter, the true reward of his labours, beyond and above the market price of his haul, is membership of what, in essence, is a secret brotherhood. The associations of master trufflers which have sprung up since the 1980s, a period of rapid growth for the trufficulture industry, are simply a formalization of an existing reality — another layer of mystery with which to wrap the package. As with other secret brotherhoods, they serve their membership in public as well as private. In France, truffle associations lobby politicians to protect the trade from alien imports, maintain prices, run competitions for truffle dogs, set rules for quality control and labelling. The Italians, always slow to regulate — not least because the luxury tax on truffle sales is around 40 per cent — are beginning to follow suit.

Regulation of what is effectively treasure-trove is notoriously difficult. The truffle has always been a trophy of the chase rather than, as with other fungi, part-and-parcel of a series of seasonal gatherings. As quarry, it's the property of the man with the gun, to be hunted in the same spirit (and using the same vocabulary) as other creatures of the wild — boar or stag or hare. Once captured, it's exhibited in the marketplace in triumph, in much the same way as a man might hang a set of antlers on the wall. And since, unlike any other quarry, it appears every year in much the same place at much the same time, its location must be kept strictly secret. Deals are clandestine, done through a middleman — possibly through two or three. As a purchaser, you can be sure that whoever sells you the truffle is not the person who found it. Such is the secrecy of the trade, in the hands of the landlord's cook — and no-one a whit the wiser. Each year, the largest and most perfect specimens attract admiration as well as a greatly elevated price. This is hard to justify in terms of the truffle's ability to enhance a dish — one grating of fresh truffle is much like any other — though when purchased by a restaurant it does wonders for the reputation of the chef.

As the trade grows more open — deals, when quantities are small, are no longer restricted to a favoured few — truffle crime is on the increase. In the season, scarcely a week goes by without reports of dawn hold-ups on mountain roads, thefts at gunpoint from the boots of cars, even of dog-knapping, a risky business, since dogs are unlikely to work for inexperienced masters and different terrains suit different breeds of dog.

James Bentley, in his observations on life in the Périgord in the 1980s, tells one such story of a local truffler in an area where incomers, purchasers of truffle woodland along with the romantic ruin that came with the territory, were either unable or too ignorant to find what lay beneath their feet. Taking matters into his own hands, the truffler simply cleared the woodlands. Suspecting the identity of the thief, the owner alerted the local *gendarmerie*, who sent a man to sort it out. The thief admitted the crime but expressed no remorse since the truffle, once ripe, is well on the way to being spoilt — and where was the sense in that in that? Both claims, announced the gendarme, were valid. The solution was obvious. The two should share the crop. The owner was outraged. "You expect me to give half my crop to a thief?" The gendarme shook his head. Not quite half: and even then only if the thief was minded to be generous and the year had been particularly good. This was, it had to be said, an excellent deal for a person who would otherwise get nothing at all. And if the owner was in any doubt of the value of the offer, he could rest assured he had the services of the canniest truffler in the region. Which, in the event, proved true.

These days — the first of the twenty-first century — the truffle has become so valuable, so universally sought after, with its prices quoted on in the internet and fetching crazy sums at international auctions, it's hard to imagine what benefit it can bring to those who search it out, the primary producers who sell it to the dealers. The news, however, is good. In its lands of origin, though the finest specimens are shipped elsewhere, it brings new prosperity to impoverished market towns. Charges are imposed for casual kerbside parking. Local restaurants and caterers set up kiosks selling truffled fast-foods to queues of eager shoppers. Local wine and liqueurs swell the profits. Also available, though truffle sellers take pride of place, are other

A local truffle market in Var in the middle of the 20th century. Not much has changed except the dealers now come in Mercedes rather than on bicycles.

products of the territory — hams, cheeses, small-production olive oils, honey, herbs — sold on the truffle's coat-tails. And for those who can't afford the real thing, there are truffle-scented pastas, fragranced rice, truffled honeys, even truffle-flavoured chocolates. What were once sleepy little villages are turned, for a few short days, into places of gastronomic pilgrimage — and never mind if the main attraction, like the customers, is imported from elsewhere.

Where there's money, there are traders, some less scrupulous than others, some of whose wares hit the marketplace without the customers knowing exactly what they are. The Chinese truffle, *Tuber sinensis,* indistinguishable in the hand from the real thing, *Tuber melanosporum,* is imported in great quantity into the markets of Europe and America. In France, where the appetite is greatest for the black, this may be as high as 60 per cent of all annual sales. Much of these imports, it must be supposed, end up in places they surely shouldn't — though when they appear as little black flecks in a pâté or a block of foie-gras, even the real thing is hard to detect. In the Christmas market at Perigueux in 2004, though locally gathered truffles were in abundance in the splendour of their tented enclave, Chinese truffles, clearly labelled — no-one

This advert in Provence hints of abundant delights in store.

could accuse the seller of deception — were also available, at a tenth of the price. And one adventurous trader, doubling her profits from the sale of Vietnamese *nem*, a popular snack in French markets, was doing a roaring trade among buyers of foie-gras fresh from the goose.

THE TRUFFLE IN LITERATURE

Literary descriptions of the truffle, until modern times, tended to the practical rather than the romantic — brief descriptions, references to certain dishes, a few recipes, botanical information of use mainly to the expert. But with moments of change — in the aftermath of war or when for some other reason we feel our civilization threatened — the literary climate shifts. In modern times, in the aftermath of two World Wars, the physical pleasures denied in times of hardship returned to favour. Great writers — among them the novelist Colette, the poet Sacheverell Sitwell and America's darling Mary Frances Kennedy Fisher — celebrated the joys of the flesh with lyrical accounts of what had so nearly gone for ever.

Mrs. Fisher, writing of Paris and Provence in the years between the two World Wars, is credited with reminding her countrymen, at a time when such reminders were sorely needed, of what might be lost if Europe's ancient civilizations were allowed to vanish. I met her once, in her grace-and-favour cottage in the Sonoma valley, bedridden but still beautiful. We talked of Aix and the violet-seller who visited the cafe where she took her morning coffee. Still there, I said, fresh from Provence myself. I'd like to say we talked of truffles. But we talked instead of quinces, and how to open a sea-urchin, and the taste of *tellines* when cooked with oil and parsley. Of truffles she wrote in *Consider the Oyster,* as she gently reminded her readers that the truffle from the tin is better than than no truffle at all: "Truffles: ah well, and ho hum. Now and then a tiny tin drifts to the top of my Christmas stocking, and is tucked away. . . I cannot believe what I have been told about soaking the fresh ones in cognac to make them more pungent, but it is true that a dry white wine will bring out the perfumes of even the canned ones, and leaves a beautiful bit of dark juice to find its place elsewhere (in a sauce. . . or down the cook's omnivorous gullet?). I have also been told, by people who sniff out truffles the way some do Picassos, that the aficionados often carry with them a packet of rosy salt, which when they are presented with a raw truffle they pinch like snuff between their thumb and forefinger of the left hand, and then sprinkle upon the strange earthy fungus. It is made of three parts of salt, two of paprika, and one of cayenne pepper. Truffles, anyone? Eggs? Rosy salt?"

In *Prisons et Paradis*, Colette delivers the most seductive of truffle talk: "At least I did learn, in the truffle country of Puisaye, how to treat the true truffle, the black truffle, the truffle of Périgord. The most capricious, the most revered of all those black princesses. People will pay its own weight in gold for the truffle of Périgord, for the most part in order to put it to some paltry use. . . away with all this slicing, this dicing, this grating, this peeling of truffles! Can they not love it for itself? If you do love it, then pay its ransom royally — or keep away from it altogether. But once having bought it, eat it on its own, scented and grainy-skinned, eat it like the vegetable it is, hot, and served in munificent quantities. Once scraped, it won't give you much trouble; its sovereign flavour disdains all complications and complicities. Bathed in a good, very dry white wine — keep the champagne for your banquets, the truffle can do without it — salted without extravagance, peppered with discretion, they can then be cooked in a simple, black, cast-iron stewpan with the lid on. For twenty-five minutes, they must dance in the constant flow of bubbles, drawing with them through the eddies and the foam — like Tritons playing around some darker Amphitrite — a score or so of smallish strips of bacon, fat, but not too fat, which will give body to the stock. No other herbs or spices! And a pestilence on your rolled napkin, with its taste and odour of lye, last resting place of the cooked truffle! Your truffles must come to the table in their own stock. Do not stint when you serve yourself: the truffle is an appetite creator, an aid to digestion. And as you break open this jewel sprung from a poverty-stricken soil, imagine — if you have never visited it — the desolate kingdom where it rules. For it kills the dog rose, drains life from the oak, and ripens beneath an ungrateful bed of pebbles . . . "

Sacheverell Sitwell, hurrying to reopen the gates to the land he loved best, describes the behaviour of diners in a restaurant in the town of Poitiers: "Arriving in the dining room during the dinner hour, my friend observed a number of persons seated at a table with their heads enclosed in pillowcases.

A countrywoman in the truffle-rich region of the northern Dordogne in the late 1970s. Many locals still truffle hunt successfully to supplement their income and guard their truffle grounds jealously.

At first, it appeared to be a meeting of the Ku-Klux-Klan; or, may be, some revival of the Holy Inquisition. But delighted sounds were emerging from those white hoods, and it was nothing more than a conference of gourmets trying out a new dish of truffles. The pillowcases were to protect their palate from contamination by the outer world."

Mirabel Osler, in search, among other joys, of the elusive truffle in the Périgord, records memories of truffle hunting in 1977: "After leaving St. Céré, we climbed up a winding road through leafless woods. The pall of winter lay over everything . . . [Reaching the restaurant], we were welcomed by

Madame Espanidel. What followed was a meal of unexpected and delectable perfection starting the best way ever, with an *omelette aux truffes*. The sliced truffles had been left in a bowl of beaten eggs to allow their mysterious smell to percolate . . . the mixture was turned into a pan of barely-sizzling butter and the eggs were cooked until they were about to solidify but hadn't quite. It was the first time we'd eaten truffles; the delicacy and scent were so indescribable we were left temporarily speechless from an experience that haunts me still . . . We never ate truffles again. However, the memory of the occasion is branded on my culinary skin even if I can no longer conjure up the taste any more than I can recall the scent."

The truffle-experience was clearly equally memorable for a certain James Peterson of New York, contributing in 1983 to "notes-and-queries" in *Petits Propos Culinaires*, the esoteric little journal started by Alan Davidson and Elizabeth David. His description of a home-made truffle-threader — a response to the instruction "lard with truffles" — is deliciously, though possibly inadvertently, sexy: "I recently was asked to truffle a capon breast for a special dinner. I invented a little device which requires only a length of metal coathanger, a piece of copper tubing and a plastic drinking straw. The piece of tubing is crimped or glued to a straightened-out, but with the hook left on the end, length of coathanger. This forms a kind of plunger. This plunger is then inserted into the straw. To use, a hole is started in the piece of meat with a larding needle. The needle is followed directly by the truffler. When the truffler has peneterated the meat and come out the other end, the plunger is pulled back and the piece of truffle inserted into the straw. The truffler is then pulled back into the piece of meat, and the straw is then slid out over the plunger, leaving the piece of truffle embedded in the meat." See what I mean?

As the truffle widened its range, reaching markets where, for the first time, it could be experienced at first hand, it attracted a new generation of literary admirers unafraid to celebrate it for what it is: delightfully aphrodisiac. To a sensualist such as novelist and magic-realist Isabel Allende, the idea of a fungi that smells like sex is irresistible. Her first experience, however, was not exactly love at first sight. The truffle's fragrance, she reports, though undeniable sexy, is similar to the scent of sweat as experienced on a warm evening in the New York subway — a perfume she had good reason to recognize since, as a penniless immigrant in the city of dreams, she could afford no other means of transport.

Nevertheless, with seduction in mind, she set out to track the truffle down. Truffle, she decided, was to be the central ingredient in a *dîner intime* to be shared with a suitor whose fame as a cook was matched by his reputation in the bedroom. The suitor however — wise in the ways of the world and considerably older than herself — had initially failed to respond to her charms. Never mind. All would change once she laid her hands on the right material. The centrepiece of the dinner was to be "an *omelette aux truffes* topped with a little cloud of red caviar, exquisitely erotic and as clear in its meaning as a gift of red roses and a copy of the Kama Sutra".

Tracking down truffles, however, was not easy in New York, though in Chile, the turbulent land of her birth, it would surely have been impossible. When she finally found the prize, a little heap of blackened rabbit-droppings in an Italian delicatessen in the Bronx, she certainly couldn't afford them. "Buy mushrooms instead," said the shopkeeper, rightly judging the depth of her purse. "I can't. I need them for — reasons." "Reasons?" Scarlet-cheeked, she nodded. "Reasons of romance." Everything changed to smiles. Drawers rattled, a tiny bottle was set on the counter. The content — olive oil perfumed with truffle — white, of course, no Italian gives a fig for black — was cheaper and just as effective. And when combined with a handful of olives - black olives — stoned, chopped and rinsed to rid them of salt and sprinkled with oil, not too much, since the effect must be subtle rather than strong — would smell and taste exactly as they should. After a few hours soaking, no-one would know the difference.

The would-be seductress went home and followed instructions to the letter. The omelette was exquisite, the fragrance perfect. The evening proceeded as planned, except for one thing. The suitor's bedroom-delivery fell well short of expectations — about as far from the real thing as, well, scraps of olive pretending to be truffles.

Deception comes with the territory. And that, as our ancestors of the wildwood knew well enough, was the attraction all along.

Black Diamonds – the Truffles of France

Auguste Breman, master truffler, inherited his small-holding from his father, who had inherited it from his father, who had inherited – and so on. His personal truffle woodland, a tangle of prickly leaved scrub oaks, well spaced, was clearly visible from road. It was safe enough, said Auguste, since he could keep an eye on it from his kitchen window, and at night, well – he flicked a battered thumb at an elderly shotgun clipped to the wall – sound travels best in darkness.

On one side of truffle territory, a patch of vines; on the other, olive trees, and these, said Auguste, each contributed to the flavour of the fungi. The rest of the terrain was given to sorgum, the crop favoured that year – 1978, as I remember – by the village co-operative. His father had valued the patch of scrub mainly for the feathered game – thrushes and partridges – which need the protection of the thorns to breed, renewing their numbers for Auguste's gun.

It was in the company of Auguste and his prick-eared mongrel that I first came across the true black truffle in its perfect state, fresh from the earth – the moment when its fragrance is at its most beguiling. At the time, I was

Every gram counts, as anyone who has purchased a truffle rapidly finds out; precise weighing is essential in such a valuable commodity.

travelling, for family reasons, through truffle territory in the depths of winter, when I took a detour through olive-country. My intention was to acquire that year's supply of untreated olive oil from an old friend, Paul Farnoux, owner and chief-operative of a venerable olive-mill whose oils, being milled from olives that have already weathered the first frosts, are sweet and mild, and very good in mayonnaise.

The mill-wheels, automated since my last visit, were turning noisily.

"*Vous aimez les truffes*?" Paul's question was casual, tossed out over the whirr of the machinery as we watched the golden liquid pouring into my gallon jar. "Do you like truffles?" he repeated, as if truffles were an everyday thing, something a person might choose to eat or not, as the fancy took them.

"*Bien sûr*, of course," I said. And lied.

I had tasted truffles to be sure, but only in processed form — as the little flecks in the smooth pink fluff of a paté, or set, like so many fine black pennies, in the crystal surface of an aspic — and neither of these, I knew, were what was meant.

"Good. I shall arrange it. You will accompany my friend Auguste. There will be truffles. They will be fresh and they will not be expensive. You must eat them immediately, as soon as you get home. You will meet me here no later than 8 o'clock tomorrow morning, and I will introduce you."

Right. No argument.

We meet as arranged. Auguste's assistant is Noireau, a little black dog, eight years old and of no particular breeding — black labrador in there somewhere, though dachshunds, cockers and setters are highly rated as truffle-hounds — with bright intelligent eyes and a very pointed nose. A good dog can fetch a million old francs, says Auguste: money a dog is more than expected to earn back for his master.

"You must treat him well." Auguste bends down and pulls a blood-gorged tick from behind a pricked-up ear. "A truffle-dog needs encouragement and love. Never beat him for failure, only reward him for success. He must be locked up the night before; no supper, no breakfast. And if there's a female dog nearby, he'll lose his concentration — don't we all? Last week, there was a bitch on heat more than a mile away. That day we found no truffles."

How do you train a dog? I enquire.

"Well," said Auguste. "The business can be short or long, depending on his natural temperament. First you feed him with bits of truffled omelette to whet his appetite and make him understand. Then you bury a real truffle in a patch of ground, show him where to look, and reward him when he finds it. Afterwards, all you need to show him is a bit of bread. I use a breadstick because it's easy to break into lengths. Noireau is clever. He measures the breadstick when we begin the hunt. When he knows there is no more left, he stops hunting."

We set off from the farmhouse on foot, down a little track in between the lines of neatly pruned vines. The plantation produces other fungi at different times of year. Summer truffles from March to June, cèpes in autumn. The tree-cover, well-spaced, includes scrub-oak, hazel and poplar. The extent is half a hectare, planted forty years earlier, pushing aside the vines in a favoured patch where oaks had already produced truffles.

The process of growth remains mysterious. And Auguste likes it to remain so. He has little time for artificiality. "You can seed the oaks with the mycelium, but it's not reliable. And in my experience, it doesn't seem to make good truffles. Healthy trees are not what you want. The worst-looking trees sometimes produce the best truffles."

It's hard to predict where and what will be found under the carpet of prickly oak leaves. One year, says Auguste, he gathered thirty kilos of truffles in a day. Another he'd be lucky to find a couple of kilos all year. In the three-month season for the black truffle, he gathers every week. "It took twenty-five years before these trees produced. You can plant a hundred trees and you will only get ten that produce — one year it'll be one which has the fungus, one year another. It's a matter of weather, too. You need rain in July and August for a good harvest the following winter, with a little sun at the right time, but still no-one can really be sure."

Noireau sets out along the line of oaks. He seems eager, like a young man looking for girls on a Saturday night. He stops, scrabbles in the earth, wags his tail, loses interest and wanders away. Auguste follows with a little pick — a sharpened stick — gripped tightly in his fist. He scrapes at the soft earth for a few moments and sniffs. There's something there, but he doesn't want to overwork the ground. He calls Noireau back, explaining that you don't let a dog scrape too long or he hurts his paws and won't work any more. Noireau

Overleaf: Truffles flourish under oaks in woodland, but with precise needs for the kind of open woodland that can be seen here in Haute Provence.

scrapes again to the left of the hole. Ah! The earth is soft. A dark shape appears. And there it is, a fine black truffle. "About fifty grams", says Auguste, lifting it gently and examining it in his hand. "Not large, but it has a good colour and scent". He cups his hand and lifts it to my face.

"There. Take a deep breath. What do you think?"

I breathe deeply. The fragrance almost overpowers me, filling my nostrils and throat with a scent so exciting, so overwhelming, so astonishingly familiar that my head swims and I have to sit down on a tree-stump. Auguste watches me. His smile is sly, knowing. "Ah. I see you recognize it." And I, a mother of four, twenty years' married, blush like a girl.

What exactly is it that makes the scent of a truffle so thrilling? Well. The chemists tell us it's the pheromones, the stuff that tells Noireau that the neighbour's bitch is on heat. There's no other way to explain the effect. It reminds some of us — not all, no doubt — of those nights when we held our first lover in our arms and learned, once and for all, what this thing they talked about in books was all about. Sex, actually — but all new-minted and carrying with it none of the baggage of later years.

I breathe deeply again. These words spring to mind: sweet almonds, ripe grapes, thyme, rosemary, juniper, the scent of heather-roots, bonfire embers after rain. After a moment, a little unsteadily, I rise. Happily for my dignity, Auguste and Noireau have moved further into the woods, no longer interested in what I have just experienced.

Noreau has found an alien scraping. There is talk of truffle thieves. The price for truffles risest highest just before Christmas, when people are prepared to pay for the festive feast, even though truffles gathered at the beginning of the season are not as good as those gathered later. January and February are best, March a little late.

For the next hour, as the sun rises over the edge of the hills, we pace the grove. Some finds are large and fine, others not quite ripe — a few well overdue, rotten as carion. One is enormous. Auguste scratches the knobbly black skin with his fingernail. Cupping his hands, he holds it out. "See that? Too many white veins. The flavour will be only moderate. You can never tell. And there. See the worm holes? Some trufflers will squeeze a bit of extra

On the trail. A good dog is worth his weight in silver. Each truffle hunter has his or her own favourite dog, and often a favourite breed, springers among them.

earth there, and into the contours — like that, so you don't see it." He demonstrates, squashing the brown paste into the crevices. "With the price of truffles as it is, every little extra is a small fortune."

The truffles are prey to a small reddish grub — offspring of a red-bronze fly, *Helomyza tuberivova* — which makes bore-holes. It seems a pity to have to share the prize with the greedy little creatures. M. Breman shrugs. "The fly which lays the eggs hovers over the truffle when it is mature enugh to push up the ground, so it is a useful way to know where to dig. It does no real harm to the truffle — you just shake them out. We have a problem with them here, but in sandy soil truffles don't seem to get them."

Auguste and the miller, Paul Farnoux, who has joined us to observe events, discuss the colour of the fly. Is it red or brown? Maybe reddish. It depends on the light. But it's the fly's behaviour which counts. The two men agree that the fly looks — well — intoxicated. As if it's just staggered home after a long night on the absinthe, or frolicking with a lady — this with a sidelong glance at me. News travels fast in the truffle groves.

"Don't believe a word he says," says the miller. "Never trust a *truffier*. Why should they tell you their secrets?"

A gun discharges and a dog barks in the distance. Noireau pricks up his ears and stops work. Some dogs won't work when there are strangers, explains Auguste. They only work one-to-one with their owners, and gunshots tell them two things — that there are strangers about and there's all the fun of the chase. Noreau reluctantly comes to heel, eats the last of his breadstick, and we take the haul home to be weighed.

In the lean-to behind the truffler's house, scales are produced. Battered but well polished, they're equipped with little brass weights. The tubers are tipped into the copper weighing-pan. Nearly two kilos. I empty my purse. Auguste smiles. We must seal the bargain with a shot of homemade walnut brandy — called noireau, like the little dog. Auguste explains it's made legally, since the Breman family have been living in the same place for generations and have special dispensation to do what they have always done. We drink the bitter brandy. Meanwhile, as the air warms up in the thin winter sunshine, the scent of the truffles is overwhelming.

"They must be eaten within three days," says Auguste. "If you mean to keep any for longer, sterilize them immediately in a bottle, sprinkled with a little salt, for two hours. But they won't taste the same and you will not have the same experience." Another sly glance. "But what can you expect? It's like marriage. Always best on the wedding night."

Ignoring this, I ask one final question. How does the *ramasseur* like to eat his truffles?

Auguste shrugs. "Me? Any way at all, but no more than two days old. In a turkey or a capon, or a chicken, or a goose. Or in the sauce for the cardoons at Christmas. Best of all, with eggs from my own hens, scrambled with my own good olive oil. Paul does a special olive-pressing just for me. We do a trade. And we tell no-one, naturally."

"One more thing," he suggests as I prepare to gather up my treasure. "You can go to the tourist markets and pay a fortune for your truffles — and still they will not be as perfect as those you have there. Or if you want to know how the real deals are done, you must go where I tell you at the time I tell you. You will not be able to buy, but you can observe. Be careful. There have been robberies, even murders."

THE PÉRIGORD BLACK AND ITS RELATIVES

Tuber melanosporum, the Périgord black (*truffe noire* — or *rabasse* in the *langue d'oc* dialect of southern France — or, in Italy, the Umbrian black, *tartufa di Norcia* and *tartufa di Spoleto*, which gives some idea of its range) is native to the scrublands of the Mediterranean regions of France, Italy, parts of Croatia and Serbia, and the greater part of northern Spain. The Périgord black is found between the 48th and 49th parallel at altitudes from 250m-1000m (720 to 3300ft) above sea level. Its season runs from early December to March, always provided that the noble nugget gets a good downpour in July and August to encourage the infant truffles to swell.

In the hand, it is roundish and lobed. It looks, when lifted from the earth, like a lump of warty charcoal. In size it varies from as small as a raisin to as big as an orange, although even larger specimens sometimes emerge. The *peridium*, the skin, is ink-black with a reddish tinge, though this can indicate a lack of ripeness. The surface, when washed, can be seen to be made up of tiny pyramids, faceted like diamonds fresh from the cutter. The *glebum*, the interior, is a deep chocolate colour, veined with tightly packed, caramel-coloured spore-material, smooth as silk.

While there are at least 60 species of truffle to be found in this region, most are of no culinary value. Apart from the Périgord black, four others are noteworthy: *Tuber uncinatum* (the Burgundy truffle); *T. brumale* (the musk-truffle); *T. rufum* (the dog-nose truffle); and *T. aestivum* (the summer truffle), also known as *truffe d'été* or the English truffle (which, being of some importance in its own right, you'll find in another chapter on page 144). A fifth, *T. moschatum*, looks much like the others in the hand but is thoroughly unpalatable: rank – disgusting, say some – and smelling strongly of petrol.

Tuber uncinatum – the Burgundy truffle – is more tolerant of soil, shade and host-tree than the Périgord black, which it much resembles in the hand though it is markedly less fragrant on the nose. It thrives on pine trees, as well as the more usual host trees. Some people hold it to be a variant of the summer truffle, though it comes to maturity later, from September to December, dovetailing into the season for the Périgord black. It's the most widespread of all Europe's edible truffles, found throughout France and beyond, in Britain and throughout Iberia, the Baltic states, Scandinavia and Russia to the north, throughout Eastern Europe, Germany, Austria, Switzerland, Italy and the territories of the Balkans, Greece and Turkey.

Tuber brumale – the musky or magenta truffle – has a black *peridium* which lacks any tinge of red and can be peeled away in the fingers. The interior, though of similar colour and texture to the Périgord black, is more loosely veined. Its territory, habit and fruiting-period are shared with it, particularly in Provence, where it can invade plantations as an unwelcome interloper. Its fragrance is tolerated by some and loathed by others – some recall loam and earth, others rotten eggs. When it appears in the markets of France, its presence is blamed on imports from Spain.

T. rufum – the dog-nose truffle – is a small truffle about the size of a hazelnut, rarely larger, with a smooth, grey-to-brown *peridium* and a delicate citrus fragrance. It's of value to the plantation owner since it appears on young trees and its presence is an indicator of *Tuber melanosporum* to come. Once the black truffle is established, the dog-nose truffle disappears. At the other end of the cycle, its reappearance is an indication of decline of the black.

Soils suitable for truffle cultivation can be identified by doing the chemistry:

A clear eye and a steady hand are essential when cleaning truffles if you are not to lose a good part of the value of your haul.

in Europe these are where truffles might be expected to emerge of their own accord. However, people whose expertise comes from observation rather than science say you will find truffles wheresoever you find the last descendants of the herds of pigs that once foraged freely through the forests of the Mediterranean *littoral*. The country people will tell you that the swineherds — an inexact description of a thoroughly random relationship — know where the truffles are likely to appear, though they can never be sure. The pigs, say their supervisors, always know where to look. Which is just to say that the truffle is not a casual crop. It doesn't come to you just because you happen to be passing. Much the same might be said of the wholesale truffle markets.

THE TRUFFLE MARKETS

A dealer's market in truffle territory is a matter of knowing exactly where and when, and even then you need to wait and watch. The secrecy has much to do with tax. The trade in the black truffle — a valuable commodity from which the state is only too eager to suck funds — is officially state-controlled. Well, Caesar must have his share. But mostly it's a private matter between, well, let's call it friends. Who knows what anyone has found beneath the truffle oaks? How much and how many, and of what quality? The general parameters are known. Everyone knows if the season has been good or bad. Official truffle prices are printed in all the local newspapers. There's even a web-site where you can check what's available and where and at what price. No doubt, when the Romans were here, the news travelled all the way home to Rome.

Richerenches is the probably the most famous wholesale market dealing in the Périgord black truffle in all France, even though it is on the other side of the Rhone valley from the Périgord, two hundred miles east towards Italy, in the foothills of the Alps. Dawn breaks late in winter in the uplands of Provence. It's already past six o'clock when the sun tips the eastern horizon, staining the hilltops and tinting the pale trunks of the eucalyptus trees. We are on the outskirts of the town, on a ring road. The market is about to begin. The *ramasseurs* — mostly elderly men, but a couple are women are *ramasseurs* too,

It's a done deal. The truffle market in Richerenches in Provence quietly hums as goods and money change hands.

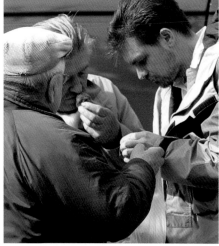

form groups, leaning nonchalantly against their vehicles' mudguards. No-one speaks. Communication is all by nod and shrug. Some have already set up trestle tables. Others, more cautious, have left their boots open to display the small, hand-held Roman scales used to confirm transactions.

The dealers arrive in diesel-powered Mercedes with Paris or Lyons number-plates, the gatherers in rusting *camionettes* or the battered *deux-chevaux* so beloved in rural France, which provide sufficient horsepower to move a man and his wife and half a ton of fertilizer. You cannot judge a man's wealth by his choice of vehicle in France: people are taxed according to visible wealth and no Frenchman who values his bank balance would ever flash a Rolex at the *fisc*. (Many an erring husband has had to give up his mistress because his wife threatens to tell the taxman all she knows!)

The sellers stamp their boots and light another fag. The two groups wait: the wholesalers in their cars, the traders beneath the trees. Meanwhile, a strange perfume penetrates the aroma of cigarettes and diesel oil — now you smell it, now you don't, like the smoke from a distant bonfire, faint but undeniable. Heavy boots — nail-studded, mud-caked — shift and stamp.

Everyone waits — for what? For some invisible signal — the arrival of the man, perhaps, who sees fair play in this clandestine gathering. One moment there's nothing but a group of seemingly aimless countryfolk in their typical *bleu de travail*, with camionettes parked at random along the road-verge and a few dealers in hunting-green with astrakhan collars. The next, the two groups meet and meld.

The trade begins. Even so, activity is kept to the minimum. Faces are unemotional. No need for the salesmanship of the retail market. The truffles remain in their containers. Buyers inspect by touch and smell, and weight. Exchanges are poker-faced — conducted rather as the Resistance must have done its business. Cash changes hands, the deal is done. Blink an eyelid, and it's gone. The street empties. Along the road, the café flips up its shutters and fills. Inside, voices are muted. The buyers take a *café-crème* with a drop of imported whisky; the sellers prefer a *demi-pression* with a Pernod chaser. The air is heavy with the scent of — well, you know exactly what. And all once, the café empties, the vehicles are gone. That's it? That's all.

Therafter, I was hooked — a confirmed truffle-lover or *"melano"*-junkie, looking for any excuse to find myself among the oaks in winter.

TRUFFLE HUNTING

Finding a truffle for yourself without assistance takes patience. It also takes luck: the good fortune to be in the right place at the right time. And even so, you have to be in the right place at the right time in the right year — that is, the one year in every four when truffles are not only prepared to fruit, but fruit in sufficient quantity to reduce the odds against someone else clearing them all away before you find them.

Some years after that first experience with Auguste the truffler and his dog Noireau, I found my first truffle for myself. It was small and not of a particularly high quality, but it was mine and mine alone. I found it in a bare patch of earth by the roadside, the only indicator of its presence a few cracks in the soil, and a slight rounding of its surface. I didn't, however, find it

Electronic scales may be less photogenic than the old-fashioned kind with weights, but at least they make sure you pay only for what you get.

without a little guidance. My guide was Paulette Villedieu, a friend of the owner of a house on the outskirts of Vaison-la-Romaine in the Vaucluse that we — parents and grown children — had rented one Christmas holiday. Paulette, a retired schoolmistress and keen botanist, and I shared an enthusiasm, since I had just finished working as a botanical artist for Kew. But when I enquired in passing if she knew of anyone thereabouts who could sell us a fresh truffle for the Christmas feast, Paulette shook her head.

"Not nowadays, no-one bothers. In my mother's day, most people had truffle-bearing trees for themselves — just as you would have a lime tree for the *tilleul*, or a patch of herbs for the *pot-au-feu*. But when I was a child, we used to find them on the way school — we walked, of course; now everyone takes the bus." She smiled. "Meet me tomorrow by the bridge. We'll take a stroll. You never know."

We met the following day by the bridge on the far side of the town. It was sunny and clear, and freezing cold. "Don't neglect the willow and elm," said Paulette, striding ahead. "Leave the oaks in case there's trouble. Use your eyes. Walk slowly and take your time."

Down a steep slope, a patch of poplar caught Paulette's eye. "There — down there. See that?"

An apron of moss, a little threadbare, ringed one tree.

"What do you see?"

I told her.

"Right. Down you go. And don't come back until you've found it."

The truffle was very near the surface, a modest little nugget which had worked itself upwards, creating a bump covered in a network of little cracks. Even so, I wasn't sure it was anything more than a lump of compacted earth until I cupped it my hand, letting the warmth release its fragrance.

"Whatever the restaurant chefs may say," said Paulette, absentmindedly examining my find. "Nothing anyone can ever do with a truffle is half as good as an omelette. The truffle has to spent the night with the eggs, of course. One night is good, two is better. But three is too long because on the fourth day the truffles lose their power. There is no point in eating a truffle on the fourth day." She scratched the dirt out of a crack in the surface of the little truffle with her fingernail. "See? A reddish tinge — that's good. Not too red, which would mean it wasn't ripe — and that would mean we'd have to bury it again and come back later when it's ripe."

Could you really do that? "Of course. Until it ripens, it's not interesting. And if you preserved it, no one would know if it was ripe or not." She shook her head severely, "There is no point in eating it *en conserve*. Only the ignorant eat truffles from a tin. And as for oil perfumed with truffle, whatever they say, it's a waste of time and money.

"All this, you must understand, is only true of *our* truffles — the *vrai truffe*, the real truffle. We have lesser truffles too, but no-one minds about those. I have no idea about the Italian truffle, the white one, which is another thing entirely and even more expensive, I'm told. But we do not have them here, so why should we want what we do not have?"

I found my second truffle — the first I had really found for myself — in the winter of 1985 in the Luberon — Peter Mayle territory for those who have read his books! — where I had volunteered to spend the first months of the year — the dead of winter — house-sitting for an artist friend. This was no hardship, since the place was large and beautiful, and full of books and

Precious cargo — black truffles cradled carefully in the hands of an expert.

paintings. The arrangement was nothing formal — a favour while I finished my first novel.

For the whole of January, I scarcely lifted my head from the page. By mid-February, as the novel started to take shape, the woodland beckoned. The château was known for its wine and there were vineyards all around. Around the house and in between the vineyards were patches of scrub that provided a refuge for birds, squirrels, rabbits and other furry creatures. There was evidence, too, of the presence of wild boar.

The woodland had been left to renew itself without human intervention more or less as it had been for centuries: there had been no commercial pressure to extend the vineyards since the wine produced from the grapes, though drinkable enough, fetched only modest prices in the marketplace. This had left a mixed woodland canopy — mostly oak, beech and hazel — undisturbed. As I walked among the bare trunks, disturbing the leaf-mould, it occured to me this might well be good territory for truffles. There were locally gathered truffles in the marketplace, and it seemed to me there might be just a chance.

That particular year had been remarkably good for fungi — warm with plenty of rainfall through the autumn, producing good crops of cèpes and chanterelles. These disappeared with the first frosts, leaving a few sodden skeletons as a reminder of autumn's plenty.

It was already well into the New Year when I took up my duties. My workday began at dawn. By midday, the lure of the woods was too strong to resist. I had been a botanical painter before I moved to the written word and I was accustomed to look for seasonal changes in the landscape. I looked for signs of spring, but the rough paths which bisected the vineyards was still iron-hard. Among the vines the earth was bare — broad swathes of ivory shading to ochre and russet.

The woodlands that edged the vineyards were easier going. And it was here that I first noticed the insects — two or three reddish mosquitoes, low to the ground. I paid no attention to the insects, concentrating on the purple shoots of dwarf field-irises, a welcome sign of spring. Next day, the flies were still there, memory stirred, and I began to take notice. The insects were lifting and landing in an untidy patch of scrub oaks. Beneath a few of the trees, one in every four or so, a wide circle had been swept as if with a rough broom in a radius that matched the canopy, about the length of a man, from the trunk outwards.

Knowing little of the basic rules of truffle-etiquette — ask no questions, hear no lies — I began to make inquiries. Were my borrowed woodlands known as truffle-territory? Had anyone found any truffles thereabouts? Shrugs, hand-spreading — not that anyone knew. Or not, with a tilt of the hat and a shift of the feet, that anyone would admit.

Other fungi of a lesser sort?

Possibly, it was hard to say.

All anyone knew was that when, some 50 years ago, the château changed hands, there was talk that truffle-rights were not included in the deed of sale. I see. Was there a resolution? These things are complicated. The mayor might know — but don't on any account mention the truffles. Not mention the truffles? Absolutely not. And anyway, even if those things which can't be mentioned had occasionally been found, it would only be in a good year when the price would be too low to be worth anyone's while.

Did I understand?

Indeed I did. I'd already been fool enough to poke a stick into the hornet's nest — only a fool would give it a stir.

The trick, as with any seasonal wild-gathering, is to know exactly where to look before you look at all. This was a lesson I learned in a remote valley in Andalucía, where I set up home with four small children and sent them to learn their letters in the one-room schoolhouse. For the eldest, seven years old and the only boy, the first day's schooling taught him how to set a trap for rabbits which were clearing out the teacher's lettuce patch. On the second-day he learned to tan a rabbit's skin to make a waistcoat. On the third day, he learned which of the roadside plants might be eaten on the way to school. And so on. To a rural community such as ours, knowing how to read the landscape was a basic skill. When we moved ourselves for one full school year to an unconverted farmhouse in the Languedoc in south-west France, the knowledge acquired at that time was once again of use.

The young scholars had to be delivered to the schoolbus at a very early hour. The bus stopped a mile away from the farmhouse. And when our track was blocked by snow or our elderly van refused to start, we walked. On the way home, I had opportunity to examine the undergrowth regularly and at

Overleaf: Golden evening light bathes a vineyard in Haute Provence. Vines and truffle oaks usually share the same territory, as they do here in the truffle-rich Tricastin hills.

close quarters. Sure enough, along the edge of the path, clearly visible in the vertical bank of red mud beneath a thicket of spiky broom-bushes, a network of little airholes betrayed the presence of hibernating snails. Snails, we had already learned from our Andalucían neighbours, were easily gathered — cropped from dried-out thistle stalks in summer — simple to prepare and good to eat. All we had to do was remember where they lived and wait for spring. Sure enough, come March, the snails abandoned their tiny burrows and began to work their way through the vegetation. And even though we knew exactly where they were, there seemed no easy way to crop them in the thick wet grass. It was my youngest daughter who discovered the secret. Too young for the big school in the town, she attended infant school in the village, where she acquired small friends who knew the territory. It's easy, said her schoolmates. Which is how we learned that every morning just before sunrise, drawn together by some strange snail-imperative, the snails would assemble on their bank and climb the broom-spikes to greet the dawn. As soon as the sun rose above the horizon, they vanished downwards swift as lightning, and hid beyond our reach. As long as we were there when the sky was reddening, the snails could be plucked from the branches like ripe crab-apples, and, when the usual preparations were completed, we could all enjoy the feast.

Meanwhile, back in the woodlands of the Luberon, I had no children with schoolmates to guide me. The pale earth between the vines was still iron-hard, flecked with shimmering shards of frost — surely it would be impossible for anything as fragile as a truffle to survive and grow — let alone to ripen. As soon as I entered the protection of the trees, the temperature rose and the leaf-mould felt soft underfoot. I moved with care, fearful of discovery, even though I wasn't in any sense clandestine since I had the owner's full permission to wander where I pleased. Nevertheless, I was well aware that in the still air of winter woods, unblanketed by leaves, noises carry for many miles — as far as the village, perhaps. And then — well, there were stories of interlopers, sanctioned or not, who'd been the accidental victims of the huntsman's gun.

Every time a twig snapped, my heart began to race. No doubt it's this element of danger — the fear of discovery for whatever reason, even that some other truffle-hunter will find out where the treasure lies, which makes the chase so thrilling. I found my reward in the narrow band of woodland which had been planted a dozen years before as a shelter-belt, protecting the vineyards from the *vent de l'altar* or east wind — the enemy of the young shoots just beginning to unfurl. I looked down and there it was — a lump of blackened vegetation, unidentifiable, unremarkable. The lump neither looked nor smelled like a truffle — at least not one that you'd pay good money for in the market-place. The casual passer-by, unaware of the message it conveyed, might have dismissed it as the rotting carapace of a walnut shell and kicked it idly into the undergrowth.

Had I not seen it where it lay, half-hidden in leaf-mould in a patch of earth that had only drawn my eye because it looked a little threadbare, I would probably have done the same. As it was, I picked it up and held it in my palm, a gentle cradling, the gesture every truffle-hunter makes when he unearths his prize. It lay there quietly in my hand, dank, evil-smelling, hollow at the heart. A spent force, its spores dispersed, only the outer shell was left — the debris which tells the tale.

That day, my modest haul — a single fragrant little nugget unearthed with a pointed stick no more than an inch or two beneath the surface — had been detected by eye alone. Thrilled by success, not wishing to disturb the habitat with ignorant digging, I looked no further. A few days later, instinctively taking a different route to avoid detection, I returned and found another.

All of which merely underlines that for the truffle, as with all other wild-gatherings, you need to know the territory — a matter of time as well as opportunity. Gathering, in the old days, was the consequence of some more essential activity — charcoal-burning, chestnut-harvesting, setting traps for meat and fur; no-one who works the land walks for pleasure. And even if the crop is as valuable as the truffle, only those who have leisure — retired folk or weekenders driving out from town — are likely to bother. The dealers alone make the kind of money that'll buy a Mercedes.

Over the next few weeks, the last days of the season for the winter truffle, my haul could scarcely be described as magnificent — no more than half a dozen in total, none bigger than a hazelnut. But all — with the honourable exception of that first empty shell — could be detected, once the spot was marked and the surface of the soil exposed, by scent alone. When the truffle hunter knows the quarry is within reach — because he knows or because his dog or pig has told him so — he'll pick up a handful of the soil and snuffle at it with his nose. If the scent is there, he'll know. It's the scent that encourages the hunter to persist, even when all other indications tell him the search is vain.

While the perfume of a fresh truffle is unforgettable – once you know it, you will always recognize it, even if only the chemical copy – experts will tell you the scent is species-specific: the white, the black, the summer, the Burgundy truffle – all have their own particular fragrance. And within the same species, no truffle is exactly identical to another. Those whose livelihood depends on their ability to nose out the difference are never mistaken. I, too, used my nose. No doubt there were many more truffles – including inferior species undetectable by ordinary noses such as mine – to be found in those woods at that time. If so, I never found them. And nor, in spite of my fears that I might be detected, was I aware of any other hunter. And there's the truth of the truffle, the reason for their scarcity, the cause of the crazy prices people are prepared to pay for them. While those who love to eat them are many, those who search for them are few – and getting fewer.

WHERE TO LOOK FOR TRUFFLES

As must already be obvious, the black truffle has not reached its position in the gastronomic hierarchy without making itself attractive to creatures other than those employed by its chief predator. Hedgehogs, badgers, foxes and members of the rat family such as squirrels and mice all find its perfume seductive enough to warrant investigation. The presence of the right host-tree surrounded by a bald patch, even if this is simply a less-furry coat of moss, combined with evidence of mammal activity, will tell you the area is worth a visit.

Since the black truffle takes between three and six weeks to reach full maturity – the moment when the fragrance is fully-developed and its presence is most apparent – there's a window of opportunity during which physical signs can be detected by the keen-eyed and well-informed, while those reliant on the nose alone won't yet be able to find it.

The best advice for those looking for truffles in unclaimed areas – those claimed will carry a notice along the lines of *"ramassage champignons interdit"* to tell you where you may or may not go – is to seek local advice. The town hall will be able to tell you of mycology societies in the area. Otherwise, consult the local chemist whose services are sought, in France, for fungi identification. Once these precautions have been taken, look for the host trees in unthicketed woodland, mark the likely areas on your map, and give yourself sufficient time to examine the terraine. Evidence of four-legged interest is a sign that even if there's nothing ripe right now, the place is worth revisiting.

THE VALUE OF THE TRUFFLE

Prosperity, the great leveller, has inflated the price in the marketplace. It is a peculiarity of random crops — succulent sea-creatures as well as fungi — that the market expands in inverse proportion to what's available. For the chef, the problem is shelf-life — the risk taken by a restauranteur when buying an unseen crop whose price is astronomical and whose viability is measured in days. For the middlemen, the problem is uncertainty of supply — though this can be mitigated by buying out of the region. For the gatherer, the problem, far less tractable, is the time it takes to gather the crop in sufficient quantity to make the trade worthwhile: however inflated the price, there's a limit to the amount any gatherer, however expert, can unearth in difficult terrain in a single day in the short season. Trufflers would be unwise to give up the day job — which is why tempers run high when the rules are breached.

So what, one might ask, are the rules? Fluid of course, and flexible. The taxman provides good reason for dealings to be secretive. Throughout the lands of the Latins, outwitting the taxman is an obligation, a sacred duty — call it the legacy of Empire, since Caesar can be held responsible for its imposition on the citizens of Rome. And if someone gets caught, everyone blames the neighbour or the wife — and usually they're right.

In France, though not in Italy, gatherings from the wild, including game, are not subject to the most collectable of taxes, TVA, on point-of-sale. Nevertheless, income tax applies to those who deal with profit — and that includes the truffle trade. My innocent question in the market-place was, I later realized, loaded with everything the *paysans* of the Luberon most disliked and feared — the imposition of unfair financial burdens on the rural workforce by the state. The Resistance in wartime France was strongly allied to the Communist party, and the divisions which date from those days are not forgotten.

The truffle is a political hot potato not simply because it provides a source of income for the finder. It was, in times when other crops failed, the only item the self-sufficient peasant, even those who owned their own land, might exchange for money. And money was needed to buy the salt that preserved perishable goods through the winter, as well as for other necessities – pins, needles, threads, ribbons – which could not be procured by barter of labour. Primary producers have always needed a middle-man, even when exchanging goods of comparatively low value: the egg-collector made his rounds and took the eggs to market, exchanging them directly for the goods the rural housewife had requested, returning to pay her in kind. The truffle trade follows the same pattern, though these days money has replaced all other forms of barter. The system ensures that the final purchaser never meets the primary producer – the gatherer – thus carefully preserving silence on what has or has not been exchanged, and ensuring only a minimal cut for the taxman.

The other factor that ensures secrecy is the Code Napoléon, which makes the purchase of land or rural dwellings by outsiders – particularly foreigners – both difficult and hazardous. You never quite know if what you're being sold is the seller's to sell – or if some other interest might suddenly declare itself, varying or otherwise limiting your ownership. So it is with woodland in which truffles are present. Such woodland is usually in association with vineyards, lavender fields and other direct competitors for space. While other wild-gathering rights are either modest – lesser fungi, berries, herbs – or easily definable – divided into so many days' hunting and so many days' fishing – truffles are both unusually valuable and totally unpredictable. In addition to the right to gather, even if this can be agreed within the family, there's the problem of knowledgeable neighbours. And even among those who know the territory, there are those who make it their business. Those who have a nose, or at least a dog with a nose. Or who are possessed of a pig. Or who are both old and a virgin – the only other qualification, apparently, which carries credibility! And woe betide the absentee landlord. Even crop-sharing rights can vanish if the gatherer decides not to admit to a haul.

The village of Lambesc, where I had, at the time of my chateau-sitting in the Luberon, fallen into the habit of filling my shopping basket at the weekly market, is not famous for anything in particular. Unless, that is, your interest

A quiet corner in Aups, in Provence, before the bustle of the market begins in earnest.

is in ladies-of-letters, when you might happen to know it was from one of its handsome *hôtels particuliers* that Madame de Sevigny wrote home to her smart friends in Paris.

Friday in Lambesc is market-day. Wise shoppers get there early. The produce comes from round about and whatever's just come into season disappears quickly. Amazingly, since we are only just into March and the winter has been hard, the week's main news is the arrival of the first baby peas, *primeurs*, from the village of Florac, a sun-trap high in the Gorges du Tarn. First and last into the market fetches the best prices. And since we are right at the end of the season for the black truffle, a few of the precious nuggets are trapped in a jar on the cheese-merchant's counter, labelled at a pricey 30 euros apiece. There will be no more this year, says the trader. A small crowd gathers. Counting my pennies, I buy. A forthright housewife tells me what to do with my prize. "Don't bother with any of those fancy sauces. Take a slice of good baker's bread — *pain de levain* — and toast it. Then rub it with garlic and good sweet oil — olive, of course, and from this year's crop. Then top it with truffle. But cut it in thick slices, not that nonsense they give you in restaurants. Salt it. Eat it. *Et voilà!*"

Just so. I, however, have other plans for my truffles. A *croustade*, perhaps, or a winter gratin. Vegetables in the market at this time of year are mainly roots and dark-leaved greens. Cabbages and leeks, cooked in the water that clings to the leaves after washing, are delicious when finished with truffle-oil. Chard, whose thick white stalks are eaten like asparagus and whose coarse green leaves can be cooked like spinach, are delicious with a truffled dressing made with walnut oil. Céléri-rave (celeriac) makes a wonderful purée when beaten with plenty of cream and an equal volume of mashed potato and grated truffle. Beetroot — when baked rather than boiled it's as sweet as honey — can be cubed and tossed with diced truffle. Turnips with their leaves (shred and steam till tender) can be tossed with garlic and olive oil and finished with grated truffle. But the bargain of the market is Jerusalem artichokes: they have a delicate flavour and texture quite at odds with their unprepossessing faces and and they work wonderfully well with the truffle.

A selection of must-haves for every truffle enthusiast, including truffle shavers, truffle oil, truffled pâté, and eggs perfumed with truffle.

NOTES ON THE PÉRIGORD BLACK

In France, grades of truffle — both preserved and fresh — are carefully regulated: "Extra" is the best, followed by "premier choix", "deuxième choix", *truffes en morceaux* — chopped truffles, and *pelures* — peelings, which are good for sauces and dressings.

The black truffle, *Tuber melanosporum,* is known in France as *truffe de Périgord, truffe Périgourdine, truffe noire, truffe des gourmets, truffe violette, truffe vraie, truffe franche*. In Italy it's known as *tartufo nero, tartufa di Norcia, tartufa di Spoleto,* taking its identity from two towns in Umbria, though it's also found in the Marche, in Veneto and in Lombardy. In Spain, it's known as *trufa negra, trufa violetta, trufa de Périgord*.

Although France is seen as its home, the world's most prolific source of *Tuber melanosporum* — identical in every way to the Périgord black — is the product of 330,000 mychorrhized oaks planted some thirty years ago on 600 hectares in the vicinity of Navaleno in the Spanish province of Soria.

"When truffles are out of season," writes James Bentley in *Life and Food in the Dordogne,* "the people of the Périgord buy truffles dried and freshen them up by soaking in Madeira." However, I have found no-one to confirm this method or even the existence of dried truffles — though the treatment certainly works with cèpes and morels. He also recommends that the contents of a partly used can of truffles may be deep-frozen and kept for up to three months.

RECIPES FOR THE PÉRIGORD BLACK

GRATIN AUX TRUFFES
Potato gratin with truffles

The robust fragrance of the truffle permeates the contents of the sealed pot, forming a fragrant black layer in the middle of the creamy slivers of potato. The idea is that the aroma is released only when the lid is lifted. If you lack fresh truffles, preserved will do (whisk the juice into the cream). Or substitute a layer of black olives, pitted and chopped, and marinated in a teaspoonful of truffle oil. Either way, make sure everyone knows what they're getting — the real thing or the copy.

SERVES 4-6

1kg (2lb) organic waxy potatoes, peeled and finely sliced
1 garlic clove (for rubbing)
A 50-75g (2-3oz) black truffle, cleaned and sliced
About 600 ml (1¼pt) whipping cream
½ teaspoon freshly grated nutmeg
A walnut-sized nugget of butter
Salt and freshly milled black pepper

Preheat the oven to 150C/300F/Gas mark 2.

Choose a casserole or gratin dish just large and deep enough to accommodate the potato slices in four layers. Cut the garlic clove in half and rub it round the dish. Lay in half the potato slices, sprinkling with salt and pepper and a few scraps of butter. Cover with a layer of truffle. Finish with the remaining potatoes. Heat the cream to boiling and pour it into the dish — you'll need just enough to submerge the potato. Dot with the remaining butter, cover with foil, shiny-side down, and cover with a tight-fitting lid.

Bake for 1½ hours. Don't remove the lid till you're ready to serve. Breathe deeply as you open the top. Heavenly, isn't it?

"On a des truffes." A young chef at the Hôtel Le Ferme restaurant at Solerieux in Haute Provence shows off the treats to come.

CROUSTADE AUX TRUFFES
Truffle tart with olive-oil pastry

A recipe from the Vaucluse, for which the crust is made with an olive-oil pastry. For the filling, preserved truffle (include the juice) can replace the fresh, and any wild or cultivated fungi can be substituted for the cèpes.

SERVES 4

THE PASTRY
250g (8oz) plain flour
4 tablespoons olive oil
warm water
½ teaspoon salt

THE FILLING
2 tablespoons olive oil
100g (4oz) cèpes (or button mushrooms), sliced
1 large onion, finely sliced
1 sprig thyme
1 black truffle (30-40g/1-1½oz), cleaned and chopped finely
4 eggs
100g (4oz) fresh goat's cheese
Salt and pepper

Work all the pastry ingredients together vigorously with the heel of your hand, using just enough warm water to form a smooth ball, which comes away from the sides of the mixing bowl. Flatten the ball a little, cover with clingfilm and set it to rest for half-an-hour, while you prepare the filling.

Heat the oil gently in a frying pan, add the cèpes, onion and thyme, and fry gently till the fungi yields up its juice and begins to sizzle. When it all begins to brown a little, stir in the truffle. Remove from the heat, pick out the thyme and leave to cool.

Preheat the oven to 200C/400F/Gas mark 6.

Roll out the pastry to fit a greased shallow tart tin – 18-20cm (7-8in) in diameter, prick all over, and bake for 10 minutes, until the pastry is set – if it bubbles, prick it again.

Meanwhile, beat the eggs with the soft cheese, plenty of black pepper and a little salt. Stir in the fungi mixture and, when the tart pastry is golden brown, spread the mixture into the tart case. Reduce the oven to 180C/350F/ Gas mark 4 and bake for 35-40 minutes until almost set, but still a little trembly in the middle.

TOPINAMBOURS À LA BARIGOULE
Jerusalem artichokes with truffles

The sweet earthiness of the roots echoes the robust fragrance of the fungi. The barigoule of the title is the dog-nose truffle, though any fresh truffle is suitable, or even mushrooms flavoured with truffle oil

SERVES 4

500g (1lb) Jerusalem artichokes
2 tablespoons olive oil
1 glass white wine
1 tablespoon pitted and stoned black olives, chopped
½ teaspoon dried thyme
1 garlic clove, finely chopped
2 tablespoons chopped parsley
1 tablespoon chopped truffle-bits (peelings)
Salt and freshly milled pepper

Boil the whole roots in salted water for 10 minutes to loosen the skins, then rub them off. (You can omit this step if the roots are very young.) Cut them into bite-sized pieces, rinse and transfer to a casserole or saucepan, with the olive oil, wine, olives, thyme and garlic. Add a little water — just enough to submerge the chunks. Season with salt and pepper.

Bring everything to the boil, turn down the heat, cover and leave to cook gently until tender — 25-30 minutes. Take off the lid and let the liquid bubble down to a little slick of shiny sauce. Stir in the parsley and the chopped truffle and allow to bubble up again. Let it cool a little before you serve it. Good with a winter salad of dandelion and chicory.

PETITE SALADE AUX TRUFFES ET CERNEAUX
Truffle salad with walnuts

Celery combines with fresh truffles, dressed with raw egg, in this elegant little salad from the Ardèche – walnut country – where it's too high and cold for olives and where nut oils traditionally replace the olive oils of the south. The walnuts must be freshly shelled, young and milky ; if not, replace with bread croutons crisped in walnut oil.

SERVES 4 AS A STARTER

4 fresh black truffles (about 25g/1oz a piece)
4 egg yolks
Salt and freshly ground black pepper
2 tablespoons wine vinegar
2 tablespoons walnut oil
2 tablespoons fresh walnuts (shell them yourself)
4-5 tender stalks celery, finely sliced

TO SERVE
Frisée endive or chicory

Brush and rinse the truffles and cut into matchsticks. Lightly beat together the egg yolks, salt, freshly milled pepper, vinegar, and oil. Turn the truffle matchsticks in this little sauce. Combine with the celery and pile on a heap of torn salad leaves – frisée endive or chicory – without dressing.

FOIE GRAS MI-CUIT TRUFFÉE
Truffled goose-liver, cooked rare

The ultimate in Christmas luxury, as prepared by goose-breeder Madame Deffaud of Le Clapier near Le Coux in the Dordogne valley. She also owns a small plantation of mycelium-treated truffle-oaks hidden behind a blackthorn hedge, although she calls on her neighbour, an accomplished *truffier*, to crop them. When choosing a fattened liver, look for firmness and paleness — ivory, lightly tinged with pink. If it looks very yellow, it'll be too fatty. Check for signs of green staining, an indication that the bitter gall-bladder has been accidentally punctured and spilled. Preserved truffle won't do, by the way; serve a little pot of truffle-butter with the toast.

SERVES 6-8 AS A STARTER

I whole fresh foie gras (1-1.5k/2-3lb)
I heaped teaspoon rough salt
I tablespoon Armagnac or brandy
I fresh black truffle, cleaned and slivered (50-75g/2-3oz)

Check the foie gras for any tubular veins; gently tug to expose them, and remove them carefully with a small sharp knife. Don't worry about making a mess of the liver: it'll reform as it cooks. Place the liver on a plate, sprinkle with the salt and brandy, and set it in a cool place overnight to drain.

Next day, drain off the juices, dust off excess salt and pat dry. Make little slits in the liver and push in the truffle slivers. Choose a terrine or loaf-tin that will just accomodate the liver. Pack it in carefully — there should be about a finger's-width of space at the top. Cover with foil, shiny-side down.

Preheat the oven to 190C/375F/Gas mark 5.

The liver must be at room temperature before it goes into the oven. Transfer the terrine to a *bain-marie* (a roasting tin which you have half-filled with boiling water) and bake for 20 minutes per 500g (1lb) of liver, till the juices run clear but are still pale pink when the liver is pierced with a sharp skewer. Allow to cool. Serve with crisp melba toast.

POULET EN DEMI-DEUILLE
Poached chicken with truffles

Literally translated as chicken-in-half-mourning, this dish gets its name from the dark veil of fine slices of black truffle slipped between the skin and the meat. One of those dishes designed to demonstrate the depth of a person's pockets, suitable for monarchs and millionaires. If you use conserved truffle, the effect will be just as pretty though the flavour will be faint, but things can be improved by adding the juice to the sauce.

SERVES 4-6

1 free-range chicken (about 2kg/4¼lb)
100g (4oz) fresh black truffle, brushed and very finely sliced
2-3 carrots, scraped and cut in chunks
3-4 celery-sticks, rinsed and roughly chopped
2-3 shallots, unskinned
Bouquet garni: bayleaf, parsley, marjoram, thyme
salt and black peppercorns

TO FINISH (SAUCE POULETTE)
3 egg yolks
150ml (¼pt) double cream

Wipe the bird inside and out. Using your fingers, gently loosen the skin by pushing between the skin and the flesh – the breast is easy, as is the top of the drumsticks. Slip thin slices of fresh black truffle between the skin and the flesh (for perfection, the bird should be entirely covered in truffle), reserving a few slivers for the finishing sauce.

Settle the bird in a roomy cooking-pot and pack the sides with the carrots, celery, shallots, bouquet garni, peppercorns and salt. Add enough water to submerge everything completely. Bring all to the boil, cover the pot and turn down to simmer. Leave to cook gently for 1½ hours, without allowing any large bubbles to break the surface, until the bird is perfectly tender. Leave it to rest in the broth while you make a little *sauce poulette*, then remove and reserve. Strain the stock and measure the volume – you'll need about 500ml (1pt) for the sauce.

To make the sauce: whisk the yolks to blend well, then whisk in a ladleful of the hot chicken broth together with the same volume of cream. Whisk in the rest of the broth. Return to a very low heat, and whisk until the sauce begins to thicken a little. Whisk in the rest of the cream and reheat gently — don't let it boil. Stir in the reserved truffle. Joint the chicken and sauce it lightly, handing the rest of the sauce separately.

ALICE B. TOKLAS' TRUFFLE TURNOVERS

Gertrude Stein is usually credited with the literary side of the cook book published by her *petite amie*, Alice B. Toklas. Ms. Toklas advises using puff-pastry and suggests frying in deep fat as an alternative to baking.

AS MANY SERVINGS AS THERE ARE TRUFFLES

1 black truffle (25g/1oz or thereabouts), cleaned, per person
Salt and pepper
1 very thin slice pork-fat or caul per truffle
1 very thin slice Cantal or Gruyère cheese per truffle
25g (1oz) pastry (flaky, short or puff) per truffle
1 egg (to gild the top)

Brush and rinse the truffles as necessary — don't peel. Sprinkle each truffle with salt and freshly milled pepper. Wrap each in a jacket of caul or pork fat, and then in a slice of cheese.

Preheat the oven to 200C/400F/Gas mark 6.

Roll out a round of pastry for each truffle, just a little bigger all round. Place a jacketed truffle on one side of each pastry circle. Damp the edges of the pastry, and fold the other side over to make a semi-circle enclosing the truffle. Brush beaten egg over the top. Bake in a hot oven for 20-25 minutes. Serve the turnovers hot, without delay.

MAGRET DE CANARD, SAUCE PÉRIGOURDINE
Grilled duck breasts with truffled sauce

For the foie-gras producers of the Périgord, the main value is in the liver, which allows the rest to be sold relatively cheap. While the legs are good for a *confit*, the *magrets* (the breast fillets) are in plentiful enough supply to serve as the dish-of-the-day in the cafés round about. If you only have preserved truffle, don't forget to include the juice in the sauce.

SERVES 4

4 duck breasts, boned but unskinned
Salt and freshly ground pepper

THE SAUCE
I tablespoon unsalted butter
I tablespoon truffle peelings or juice
I tablespoon finely diced Bayonne ham
I tablespoon diced shallot
I tablespoon diced carrot
I tablespoon finely chopped celery
sprig thyme, bayleaf
I teaspoon flour
I glass red wine
750ml (1½pt) strong duck or chicken stock
Salt and pepper

TO FINISH
I tablespoon matchsticked black truffle
½ tablespoon unsalted butter

Lightly score the duck-skin without going through to the flesh. Season the meat on both sides and reserve while you make the sauce.

Melt the goose fat in a heavy copper-based pan. Add the ham, shallot, carrot, celery, bayleaf and thyme and fry very gently for 20 minutes or so, until soft and lightly caramelized — this is a basic *Mirepoix sauce*. Sprinkle in the flour and stir over the heat till the mixture browns. Add the wine to halt the cooking process and allow to bubble up, whisking till smooth. Add the stock, bubble up, turn down the heat and simmer gently for 30 minutes, till reduced by a third. Sieve, pressing to extract all the flavour. Taste and adjust the seasoning, and leave on the side of the stove.

Heat a heavy iron grill-pan till smoking. Drop the seasoned magrets skin-side down on the hot metal and wait until the fat softens and begins to run and the skin gilds — 3-4 minutes. Turn carefully and sear on the other side, allowing another 3-4 minutes. Remove the pan from the heat and leave on the side of the stove for 5 minutes for the meat to firm and settle — duck breast should be pink and juicy, but not soft and red.

Meanwhile reheat the sauce, whisk in a few scraps of butter to add flavour and gloss, and stir in the matchsticked truffle. Transfer to a warm sauceboat.

Slice the duck breasts on the diagonal and finish with the sauce. Serve with *pommes Sarladaise* — thick-sliced potatoes cooked very gently in goose fat with sliced shallots — or sauté potatoes.

OEUFS BROUILLÉS AUX TRUFFES
Scrambled eggs with truffles

The truffle hunter's breakfast. Preserved truffles, self-evidently, won't do for the overnight aromatization of the eggs. A passable imitation of the dish can be achieved with a handful of black olives, pitted, chopped and soaked for a few hours in a teaspoon of truffle oil but take care to warn your guests that they're not about to experience the real thing.

SERVES 4

8 perfectly fresh free-range eggs
1 fresh black truffle (about 50g-75g/2-3oz), cleaned
100g (4oz) unsalted butter
Salt and pepper

TO FINISH
25g (1oz) unsalted cold butter, diced small

Bury the truffle in the eggs overnight in a stoppered jar. Next day, brush any soil off the truffle – don't rinse unless this is really necessary – and cut into fine matchstick slivers. Crack the eggs into a bowl and fork them briefly to blend – don't beat. Season with salt and pepper.

Melt the butter gently in a heavy pan. When it froths – don't let it brown – add the matchsticked truffle and toss it over the heat for 1 minute, no more. Stir in the eggs and cook the mixture very gently, moving the base with a wooden spoon, till it forms creamy curds. Remove from the heat immediately and dot with little flakes of cold butter. Serve on warm plates, with fresh baguette or croutons fried crisp in butter.

OEUFS À LA COQUE TRUFFÉS AU SEL ROSÉ
Truffled soft-boiled eggs with rosy salt

Paulette Villedieu of Vaison-la-Romaine, whose recipe this is, says her father liked his truffled eggs cooked the way his maman used to make when he was a toddler: soft-boiled, with toast soldiers. Accompany them with Mary Frances Kennedy Fisher's rosy salt.

SERVES 3

6 perfectly fresh free-range eggs
1 fresh black truffle (nothing else will do), cleaned

ROSY SALT, TO SERVE
3 teaspoons *fleur du sel* (sea-salt)
2 teaspoons paprika
1 teaspoon cayenne pepper

Unsalted butter

Leave your truffle with the eggs overnight in a stoppered jar; during the hours of darkness, the shells, being porous, will soak up the scent like a sponge.

Next day, carefully prick the end of each egg. Bring a large pan of water to the boil, and slip in the eggs, which should be at room temperature. Allow 3-3½ minutes, depending on size. Remove immediately and give each shell a gentle tap to crack it and stop the cooking process.

Present the eggs on plates — in France, egg-cups are rarely encountered — with the sliced truffle, a little heap of rosy salt (just blend the ingredients together) and a small pat of unsalted butter. Encourage participants to sandwich the slices together in pairs with butter, finishing with a pinch of salt. Take a mouthful of truffle, a mouthful of egg — sheer heaven.

OMELETTE AUX TRUFFES PÉRIGOURDINE

James Bentley in *Life and Food in the Dordogne* suggests this truffle omelette, as made by his truffle-gathering neighbour, which includes a little glass of Monbazillac, the sweet wine of the Périgord. Goose-fat — naturally enough since this is goose-country — is used rather than butter. Any ordinary brandy can be used instead of cognac, also a local product, and the wine could be replaced by a Moscatel or a Madeira. Preserved truffles can replace the fresh — add the juice and cook it down.

SERVES 4

50g (2oz) truffle pieces
2 tablespoons goose-fat (or unsalted butter)
1 tablespoon cognac or other brandy
4 tablespoons Monbazillac (or other dessert wine)
8 large free range eggs
Salt and freshly milled black pepper

Dice the truffles small. Gently melt 1 tablespoon of the goose-fat in a small pan and add the diced truffles. Season with salt and pepper. Add the brandy and the wine, bubble up for a moment to evaporate the alcohol, cover loosely and leave to simmer gently until the liquid has completely evaporated — about 10 minutes. Remove and allow to cool.

Blend the eggs using a fork — not too thoroughly — and stir in the truffle mixture.

Heat a large omelette pan with the rest of goose-fat. When it's very hot, pour in the eggs, tipping the pan to coat the base. As soon as the edges set, use a spatula to draw the soft curds into the middle, allowing the rest to run to the sides. As soon as it begins to look creamy rather than runny, quickly turn one side over the other and flip the whole thing out onto a warm plate to make a neat, fat bolster. The whole business should take no more than 90 seconds. Serve immediately, while the interior is still juicy.

OEUFS À LA TRUFFE À LA CRÈME
Eggs with truffles and cream

The most exquisite of truffled egg dishes, as served at La Table du Comtat in Seguret, Vaucluse, where I had it for one of those benchmark birthdays most of us try to avoid. Seguret has a truffle market every week in the season. For this dish, flash-frozen truffle is the only possible alternative.

SERVES 4 AS A STARTER

50g (2oz) fresh black truffle, cleaned
4 large free-range eggs
100ml (4 fl oz) single cream
Salt and pepper
25g (1oz) butter
2 tablespoons pinenuts

Slice off the tops of the eggs carefully with a sharp knife. Separate the yolks from the whites. Combine the egg yolks with the cream and season with salt, pepper and truffle juice, if the truffles are canned.

Beat the whites to a stiff foam with a little salt.

Reserve four thin rounds of the truffles and slice the rest into matchstick strips; place them inside the eggshells. Melt the butter and toss the truffle slices over the heat for a couple of minutes. Season and reserve.

Pour coarse salt into an oven-proof dish. Arrange the eggshells on the salt, pressing them so they stand up. Pour as much yolk and cream mixture into the shells as they will hold.

Bake for 2 minutes in a preheated oven at 180C/350F/Gas mark 4. Remove and top with the whisked white, stuck with a few pinenuts. Return to the oven for another 2 minutes. Lift off the lids, tuck in the truffle slices, and replace the lids. Serve with toast-soldiers, as for plain soft-boiled eggs.

Ivory Princesses –
the Truffles of Italy

The rich man's truffle, the Piedmont white (*Tuber magnatum*) has a short season (three months in autumn); a demanding growing habit (chalky clay in landslip territory with plenty of ground-cover); a limited range (Piedmont, Tuscany, Emiglia Romagna, including the estuary of the Po and the Marche in Italy, plus the north-west corner of what was once Yugoslavia and a small slice of southern Switzerland). Once formed, the truffle comes to maturity in a single day – if not found within a week, it's over the hill (by comparison the Périgord black takes a leisurely month to six weeks to reach its full potential).

In Piedmont, in the Langhe and Monferrato regions where most of the region's truffles are gathered, it's said that "*magnato*", the name by which the Piedmont white is more familiarly known, comes to maturity after the third moon after the September rains, and by the first frosts it's gone. Officially, the season runs from mid-October until the end of December, though in frost-free areas it can still be harvested at the end of January. It was first identified botanically as *Tuber magnatum* 'Pico' – Pico being the name of the botanist who first described it in 1798 – when its virtues as a tonic, fortifying

White truffles wrapped in gingham nestle in a basket in the market at Alba in northern Italy.
To buy this stash would cost you a small fortune.

and blood-thickening, were recommended in a dissertation delivered to the Faculty of Medicine at the University of Turin.

In the hand, the colour of "*magnato*" is ivory to chestnut. In shape, it has the unpredictability and smoothness of river-bed pebbles. The best — those which fetch the highest prices — are perfectly spherical, since lobes and folds can harbour decay. The interior, the *glebum*, is cream to ivory to dark brown with darker veining. When symbiotic with lime or oak, the flesh is pink with a reddish tinge, while those that grow on poplar are cream to ivory and can have a greenish tint. Size is good — one large truffle is always preferable to two smaller ones of the same weight — though anything larger than a hen's egg, prized by restaurateurs who need to impress their customers, will carry a premium out of proportion to its worth. If the truffle is fresh, the exterior, the *peridium*, will be lightly dusted with what looks like powder but is in fact the natural bloom on the skin. Any sign of beading with moisture will tell you the truffle is already in decline.

Now for the feel and the fragrance. Take the truffle in your hand and raise it to your nose. At the same time squeeze very gently to make sure the flesh is firm. There should be a little springiness but no softness. Inhale the fragrance: this should be overwhelmingly pungent, clean, sweet and fresh, and without the slightest hint of petrol or gas — a classic sign of decay. Unless you have gathered it yourself and can vouch for its freshness, consume it on the day you buy it. If this is impossible, wrap it in a scrap of clean linen, pop it in a glass jar — no rice, as so often advocated, unless it be a few grains in the bottom of the jar to absorb any moisture — and keep it in the salad compartment of the fridge for three days at most. As for the cooking, though traditional recipes suggest otherwise, the white truffle should never be cooked at all but shaved very thinly, in ribbons, onto something hot and preferably buttery.

TRUFFLE HUNTING IN ITALY

The appeal of one member of the truffle species, one might think, is pretty much like another, since all depend for their attraction on the same chemical cocktail. Or so I thought, until one sunny day in mid-November in the Siena hills when, for the first time, I encountered a white truffle straight from its bed. I had, it must be admitted, a little professional help, a rendezvous arranged by Nancy Jenkins, author of *Flavours of Tuscany* (the definitive work on the cuisine of Tuscany), with a licensed *trifolao* — the dialect name for a truffle hunter — in the *Creti Sienese*, a clay-caked limestone ridge that is characteristic of the this part of Italy.

We meet, as arranged, at a crossroads — anonymous, unmarked, the perfect place to meet in truffle territory. A truffle safari with a licensed *trifolao* is a perfectly respectable way for a *trifolao* to ensure a modest return on his labours, no matter what the haul. And never mind if finds can sometimes seem a little too opportune and you're unlikely to visit anything other than the most accessible gathering grounds.

Our guide, dressed from head to foot in hunter's patchwork green, awaits us at the wheel of his mud-caked Landrover. By his side is his companion *trifolao* — "We work in pairs," he says, by way of introduction. His companion, short and stocky, has burgundy-tinted hair quite at odds with her muscular build and carries a stout stick. She, too, is dressed for the jungles of Vietnam. Gazing over the tail-gate are three woolly-coated dogs of medium size, with floppy ears, their bright pink tongues lolling from short, thick muzzles.

It is already mid-morning by the time we reach our meeting place. The hour suggested was somewhat to my surprise, since I have already been told the proper time for a foray is during the hours of darkness for reasons that vary from the romantic (truffles are formed where moonbeams fall on tree-roots) to the practical (dogs pick up scents more readily at night) to the downright commercial (the truffler needs to keep the source of his haul to himself).

Yet here we are in bright broad daylight. The reason is soon made clear. It is illegal to hunt for truffles in Italy at night. This, our legally licensed guide explains severely, is to ensure that unscrupulous, illegal or careless gatherers are prevented from spoiling the truffle grounds — a greater danger than revealing where these are. Traditional gathering grounds, in any event, are well known to everyone in the trade — and anyway, nobody can find them without a dog which knows the territory. There are are some 8,000 licensed *trifolaos* such as ours in the truffle regions, all of whom have passed the knowledge-tests and paid the fee officially required before a *trifolao* can hunt.

So much for midnight raids. We drive in procession along narrow tracks past stone farmhouses dwarfed by slender cypresses, straight as candles, green and dark against the winter landscape. Branches are bare at this time of year, although the oaks — deciduous trees that keep their frost-dried leaves throughout the winter — are flagged with brown. Here and there are pomegranate trees with fruits that gleam like Chinese lanterns. Alongside the road, among the stripped-out apple and cherry trees, hang quinces, yellow globes furred with white, and medlars like little brown oak-apples with star-shaped tips.

We roll to a halt at the edge of a track on the prow of a line of little eminences, like upturned sugar bowls, punctuated by *calenque* — snow-white cliffs of a startling brightness. The line is not continuous since some of the sugar bowls have been flattened to make fields, with the tops of the hills spread in the valleys — laborous work with pick and shovel. The precipitous slopes left in place are known to yield *"magnato"*, though, explains our guide, the steepness and roughness of the territory is not for amateurs like us.

The dogs, released from their mobile prison, are eager for the hunt. The source of their enthusiasm — pairs of dainty little double hoofmarks — leads down towards the valley floor. *"Cingale* — wild boar," says our guide grimly, prodding the small depressions. At this time of year the pigs are rutting, and that distracts the dogs, our guide explains. In this particular region — though not in Piedmont, where the *cingale* have been eradicated — the presence of wild boar is an indication of truffle territory. We set off behind the furry-coated dogs, already halfway down the slope. The track beneath our boots is the colour of milky chocolate, sticky as toffee. On either side, banks of red clay are cut with seams of the milk-white chalk held in place with broom bushes (*Genister*), the emblem of England's warrior kings.

From the naked spikes of the broom, as I remember from my days in France, can be gathered snails at dawn in springtime. Is this also the case in Italy, I enquire eagerly? "It is." Our guide reveals himself is a man of few words, a characteristic of the country folk of the territory.

I persist. "At this time the snails are burrowed in for the winter, are they not? In France they say that when the snails dig deep, the winter will be harsh."

Our *trifolao* nods dismissively. "That may be so in France, where they do things differently and *"magnato"*, of course, is not present". For *"magnato"*, the snails are both good and bad, says the taciturn one, warming to his subject. Their subterranean activity aerates the clay, allowing moisture to enter and nourish the truffle. In spite of this useful work, the snail is also a predator, accounting for the circular bites that appear in otherwise perfect truffles,

Truffle country in spring on the slopes of the Umbrian hills.

lowering their price. "Another major predator, a serious problem, is the hedgehog. It's protected in Italy so there's nothing to be done. It leaves series of scratched-out patches bunched together in one place, as if the first burrowings were unsuccessful."

Even more destructive, he says, poking the little depressions again with his stick, are the wild boar, which churn up the earth and make a terrible mess. But the most disastrous of all, adds our *trifolao*, is the irresponsible unlicensed truffle-thief who uses a rake and a spade rather than the traditional neat little pick to extract the truffle from its bed. "The mycelium is very delicate. Once broken, it cannot be repaired. Disease gets in and the whole gathering grounds are put at risk. How do we prevent this? Vigilance. If the thief is local, everyone

knows everyone else's business and you know who the culprit might be. But when the thieves come from elsewhere, immigrants and so forth — well, it's a problem in the countryside as well as the city."

In areas where there is no cultivation, our *trifolao* explains, anyone who has passed the exam and paid the licence fee is permitted to gather. Others, such as the one we are about to inspect, are reserved for a particular *trifolao* by arrangement with the landowner — in this case, the farmer whose tractor can be seen on the far slope moving steadily along the ridge against the sky, turning the clods of terracotta earth in rich parallel waves of chestnut and chocolate. *"Magnato"*, unlike most other truffles, likes a little movement in the soil. Since its preferred habitat is chalk-based clay, which — as can be observed on our boots — is sufficiently impervious to both air and water, the soil needs to be aerated by regular minor landslips, such as those produced by the plough. And these valleys, rich and fertile, have been ploughed for ever — since the days when oxen tilled the earth with wooden ploughshares. Among the dark furrows drifts the debris of more deadly encounters — Etruscan swords, Greek helmets, Roman shields, the bleached bones of long-dead warriors. These are collected, polished and displayed in modest municipal museums which, though nothing much to boast about, have proved, like the truffle harvest, to be a draw to the tourists, and a useful source of extra revenue.

Our working companions — Jessie, Susie and Lila — are *largatos*, water-dogs bred for the hunt. One is pure-bred, the other two are half-breeds, though all three are curly coated, like poodles. At the end of the track, a line of poplars marks the stream's edge, dense with brambles beneath the bare branches of willow, elder and silvery poplars, tall and graceful. Along its slippery banks truffles are found. *"Magnato"*, the only truffle found in this terrain, likes sticky clay and plenty of shade. Between the patches of vegetation can be seen white seams worn by the passage of water.

The stream in the valley floor has cut itself a deep ravine. Swelled by the autumn rains, its pace is swift. The dogs splash noisily through the water, encouraged by cries of *"Vai, vai, Susie, Jessie, Lila. Che, che."* In between the encouragement, the *trufolaos* make a strange clicking noise, like a crow encouraging its chicks. "Frost is good," says the taciturn one, turning over a

Ready for the hunt. An octagenarian, known locally as the King of the Truffles, who has been truffling successfully above Norcia, in Umbria, for more than 70 years.

crisp nest of grass. Susie is just a learner, the expert is Lila. Jessie, though showing promise, is young and her enthusiasm needs to be tempered.

"*Vai, vai.*" Lila has found something. She scrapes and scratches, snorting with pleasure. Our *trifolao* gently pulls her back. He pushes his pick into the earth, removes a clod. The earth is transfered to the hand. Air and warmth release the fragrance – faint as yet, but unmistakeable.

"Good girl." He pats Lila's head, transferring a little scrap of biscuit to her mouth – blink and it's gone.

"Let's see."

The pick goes back into the little trough. Nothing is yet visible. By now all three dogs must be restrained. Another delicate scratch, and there it is – an ochre-coloured pebble no bigger than a walnut, no different to the eye than any other pebble. But then, once released to the air, an astonishing perfume soars.

I lean closer, anxious to discover how miracles happen. The truffle, it seems, has made itself a tiny hollow, a little cave which exactly follows its own contours. The narrow margin of air that separates the living organism from its impermeable bed is so exact, so precisely carved as to mirror its form, that you almost believe it's not there at all. But there it is, a cocoon of air and warmth trapped in a watery cradle of clay, a miniature incubator that has allowed the living organism to come to fruit.

Its aroma has been described as a blend of perfect Parmesan and the freshest young garlic – fragrances which are indeed discernible, though I'd say that these are most evident when the fungus is a little past its best. Just lifted from the earth, there's a spiciness there, a breath of fennel pollen or crushed aniseed; a sea fragrance – oysters, salt-breeze, seaweed – and a leafiness, a peppery freshness, like the first green buds of spring. And beneath it all the elusive pheromones, the real reason for every truffle's appeal, work their subversive magic.

Next time she finds one, Lila is too quick. One gulp and it's gone. We inspect the silky bed. Nothing remains but the perfume. "*Buon apetito,*" says our *trifolao* resignedly, raising a handful of earth to his nose. You may verbally chastise but you must never beat a truffle-hound. We continue on our way. The hedgehogs have been busy. Three other tubers are unearthed, small but satisfactorily fragrant, all slipped quickly into the *trifulao*'s ample poacher's pocket without discussion.

The hunt is over. Our *trifolao* is anxious to return to base. This is his truffle-shop in San Giovanni d'Asso, run as a sideline by his daughter who, since he is a widower, takes care of business in his absence. In fact, he says, she will make a meal for us if we're prepared to wait.

The daughter, a young woman of even fewer words than her parent, explains what we already know: we must wait. The house speciality, we can rest assured, is worth the wait. To do justice to the truffles we are about to eat, the *linguine*, fine strips of all-egg pasta, must be freshly made elsewhere. Her father will fetch them when they're rolled.

Her father, however, has bigger fish to fry. He has to catch the post. Quite casually, with no more ceremony than might be applied to a sack of potatoes, he tips onto the counter the contents of a gallon-jar. All the truffles are perfectly spherical, unmarked, each the size of a baby's fist. Our *trifolao*, raising one perfect egg-shaped tuber to his nostrils, allows himself a smile. "Wonderful, isn't it? I couldn't do this on my own — no-one could. It would take a month for one man to gather so many, even in a good year in the best grounds. And then he couldn't sell them because the truffles would no longer be worth eating. So it has to be like this. The dealer is essential. There's no crop without a dealer." Their destination, Germany — the restaurants of Bonn, Berlin, Munich, Frankfurt — where the clients can afford the price. The morning's activities, he adds, is a sideline, an exercise in public relations. The real money is in the sale of first-class truffles at the highest price. A chef can charge ten times over whatever he pays: if the perfume is right, the punters will pay.

Sant'Angelo in Vado is one of four market towns servimg the mountain communities of Catria e Nerone, a population of independent *contadini* scattered over some 500 square kilometres of wild ravines and densely wooded hills in the rocky foothills of the Appenines. All four towns — the others are Apecchio, Piobbico and Aqualagna — celebrate the Piedmont white in its season. All have truffle festivals, truffle shops and restaurants specializing in truffle dishes.

The road between Sant'Angelo and Aqualagna winds through the heart of truffle country, following the curve of the hills, offering a deer's-eye view of the wooded slopes across the valley. And if, travelling between the two in search of the elusive tuber, you should spot a camionette or one of the elderly

Overleaf: The rich red soil of the Marche hills plays host to some of the best Italian white truffles, and black ones too for good measure.

saloons parked by a deserted roadside, far from any signs of habitation, the probability is the occupants are after truffles. And if you pause in your journey to inspect the hillsides across the valley, you may just catch a glimpse of a man with his dog. Or you might even spot, tucked into a secret fold, neat rows of pale-trunked poplars, an experimental planting of host-trees infected with *T. magnatum*, one of just a hundred or so in all Italy. The white truffle found here, in the district of Catria e Nerone in the region of the Marche, while undeniably "*magnato*", the rich man's truffle — known elsewhere as the Piedmont (or Alba) white truffle and identical to it in every way — is also claimed as the truffle of Aqualagna.

"'*Magnato*' is three times the price of "*melano*" (the colloquial name for the Périgord black) because it's three times as powerful," explains Giorgio, the field-scientist who runs the experimental trufficulture laboratory in Sant'Angelo-in-Vado which has been working on the Aqualagna truffle. "We know because we work with them both all day. Our "*melano*"-expertise comes from France, but we are the experts on "*magnato*". And I can tell you that after a "*magnato*" day, we have to open the windows before we go home so the atmosphere can calm down. We laugh, of course, but that's the truth."

Caterina, the young woman in charge of press relations for Sant'Angelo's annual truffle festival, giggles. Caterina has already confessed to having no liking for truffles — she is, she says by way of explanation, from the Veneto — and nor, she says, does her husband, and he is from the Vado. Her blushes are not uncommon. There's something disreputable about a substance which draws such public enthusiasm, whose underlying message is, well, a little uncivilized.

I, on the other hand, need to know the detail from Giorgio.

"You're talking pheromones?"

"*Certo*. It's not too long since they did the trials in Britain. They took two groups, ten men in each — twenty in all. The first ten were shown a picture of a truffle, then they were shown photos of beautiful models and asked to rate them for sex-appeal — so many points for this and so many for that. The second group was given a truffle to smell before they were shown the pictures. With the first group, the response was mixed. With the second, the ones who actually had the truffle in the hand, the response was 100 per cent — all the girls got the highest possible rating."

He laughs. "Here in the lab we knew exactly what the result would be. In Italy they've always had a reputation as an aphrodisiac, which is why they were always sold to the rich. But nowadays, everyone can afford a little now and then. Demand increases every year and we're under increasing pressure to produce results with the white. Success is still relative, but it's a start."

The agrobotanists are quietly optimistic. While the Périgord black (*T. melanosporum*) and the summer truffle (*T. aestivum*) are already well established as a commercial crop, providing the lab with its main source of income from the sale of mycorrhized saplings, until now the white has proved remarkably hard to propagate. Success, however limited, is good news for everyone involved. Even the taxman stands to gain, since for the first time a crop previously impossible to quantify will be taxed at point of production — a situation which may not sit well with the growers, and probably even less so with the dealers.

Enough of tax. And how, I enquire, does Giorgio himself like to eat his truffles? He smiles. "With cheese of course, just as they like it here; "*magnato*", of course, grated over the pasta. Maybe with a well-aged Parmesan — not pecorino, that's too strong — or melted fontina. Something delicate, not too overwhelming, but vigorous enough to bring up the scent of the truffle without killing the fragrance. There's a restaurant in Aqualagna which knows exactly how to do it."

THE WHITE TRUFFLE MARKETS

In Aqualagna, the *cantina* for the annual truffle *fiera* are not yet assembled in the piazza. Giorgio's recommendation turns out to be the only restaurant in town which opens its doors on a Tuesday — each has its allotted days for closure to give the others a chance. On the menu, as Giorgio promised, is pasta with *tartufi bianchi*. My waitress is careful to establish an understanding: "Today it's 18 euros for the white. We set the price ourselves. Is that all right?" When the pasta arrives — ridged, chewy, and about the length and shape of a baby's finger — it's bathed in melted *fontina* gritty with tiny scraps of summer truffle. And then, floating overall, light as swansdown, is a thick soft blanket of semi-transparent ribbons, greenish in colour, of "*magnato*" from whose delicate surface rises the unmistakeable fragrance.

That weekend I return for the fair itself. While Sant'Angelo's *fiera* is the most famous — a national event, you're sure to spot a dozen politicians and just as many movie stars – Aqualagna's fair is a more modest affair. A single line of stalls encased in white canvas borders one side of the piazza, while a row of fast-food kiosks, half-a-dozen or so, lines the other. At 10am on the final Sunday, a sunny day in early November, only a handful of the hardiest truffle-fanciers wanders among the stalls, but by midday the piazza is packed. The stall-holders also stock truffle-related products – aromatized rice, oils, sauces, polenta. Aromatized products are the bread-and-butter of the truffle trade; there's no question they're far easier to sell when the scent of the fresh truffle clouds judgement. For the serious punters, "*magnato*" are marked at between 2,500 and 3,500 euros a kilo, while the last of the summer black costs 400 euros for the same amount.

Among the stall-holders, I canvas opinions on reasons for variations in colour of their wares – some appear very pink, others have reddish patches and some have blackened seams. Irina, the most helpful of the stall-holders, tells me the terrain matters less than the host-tree – and it's this that dictates the quality and colour of the truffle. Reddish marks on the exterior, the *peridium*, indicate an oak-tree truffle: scratch the surface – she demonstrates with a finger-nail – and you'll find the interior reddish. And a reddish colour, for those who are not obliged to present them in a restaurant, indicates high quality, as does the blackening of the exterior which distinguishes a truffle grown in a charcoal area, the burnt-out patches left by summer brush-fires.

By one o'clock the kiosks are doing good business in truffled take-aways cooked to order and sold by portion on paper plates – the choice is black or white truffle (and priced accordingly), the vehicle might be home-made all-egg pasta, potato gnocchi, soupy polenta or *crecie*, flaky pancakes lightened with lard and rolled round a truffle-sprinkled frittata. "We're home cooks over here. We only do it because we enjoy it," says Irina's mum, handing over a generously truffled heap of gnocchi. "And once a year is all it takes."

Prices in the market-place reflect the seller's need to cover the tax payable at point of sale – on luxury goods, including truffles, a whopping 40 per cent. Since the primary supplier, the finder, always works with cash, the dealer has to pay at least a percentage of the full tax, the local VAT equivalent,

There's good money to be made in the by-products of truffles and every market in the truffle regions of central Italy is plentifully stacked with truffle goods.

and his prices have to be high enough to cover the cost of the original deal because he can't reclaim what the *contadino* hasn't paid.

In Sant'Agata, as elsewhere, the seller's pitch is international. A single perfect truffle is raised gently to the nostrils, inhaled, the eyes roll heavenwards and. . . Well, I buy, of course I do, an ivory bauble the size of a walnut, fragrant and perfect. The price is 50 euros — a bargain, let no man tell me otherwise — bought as a gift for my guides to the region, Franco Taruschio and his wife, Ann. Franco, born and bred in the Marche, and Ann, a bright-eyed, down-to-earth Yorkshirewoman, were until lately chef-proprietors of the Walnut Tree restaurant in Abergavenny in South Wales, my own home territory.

"You need not think you'll ever be cheated," says Franco, examining my prize with a practised eye. "All sales are regulated, tax has to be paid and receipts are checked at random. Anyone involved in an unrecorded sale of any kind has to to pay a heavy fine — buyer as well as seller." He shakes his head. "In private — well, this is Italy."

The "*magnato*" of the Marche are as good as those of Alba — better, one might say, since the truffles you buy in the region are unlikely to have come from elsewhere. In the days when he ran the restaurant, he continues, he and Ann made regular trips to the region to buy his supplies direct from a *contadina*: "A remarkable woman, as tough as a man. We'd meet at a certain time in a certain place — somewhere we couldn't be observed. And she'd let me know she had an ancient pistol in one pocket and the money in the other. But her truffles were always reliable."

Reliability, to a man of the Marche, is of paramount importance. The people of the Marche, says Franco, have a reputation for seriousness. "All Italy knows we lack frivolity. The *contadini* because the life was harsh and the landlords were hard men. Even in a bad year, they took half the crop, and that meant the *contadini* starved. When I was a boy, all this — the irrigated pastures, the new farm-buildings, the crops of sunflowers sold for money, the olive trees in rows — everything you see today, all this was subsistence farming. No-one owned their own land. We were share-croppers. The landlords lived on the hilltops and the families were always feuding. There was a lot of hate and hardship, and talk of ancient wars.

The mountains in the Marche region are rich in truffles, and truffle hunting is serious business here.

"And then, when I was still only a child, there was another war and the soldiers came. Which soldiers? Ours, yours — Americans, Germans, British, Italians — it was all the same. We were the *contadini*. They took our houses and everything we had and we lived in the fields, and hid in the woods and waited. We ate whatever we could find. There were soldiers everywhere. The Germans were the most impressive. I remember a German officer, stripped to the waist, who rode his horse like a god. He was so beautiful and so full of life that we could only admire him, even when we knew he just had killed a man we knew, a neighbour, who had hidden the horse in the hayfield. Human nature is like that. We admire what's beautiful when we see it. We cannot help ourselves. We all wanted to be like him as he rode away in the sunlight. Even

though I had no admiration for who they were and what they did. As a young man, I was a Communist. We were poor. What else could we be?

"Truffles? I don't remember. Perhaps. Among the poor, there was no tradition of eating them when there was a possibility of exchanging them for money. It's only over the last ten years that ordinary people have become really interested. And now it's crazy — it's become like a drug. Thirty years ago you'd go to a truckers' pull-in, and if you wanted truffle with your pasta, they weighed one out for you and grated it on — as much as you wanted or you could afford."

The road that leads into the little town of Sant'Agata Feltria in the hills above Rimini is narrow and winding, single lane, a drive of an hour or more. Distance and difficulty is no deterent to those who seek the mighty *"magnato"*. At four o'clock on a Sunday evening in mid-October, a 13-kilometre stream of traffic — cars, motorbikes, lorries, buses — has formed queues in both directions. The hills are small, sugar-loaf-shaped, edging the valleys. Small-holder territory, rocky and marginal, ideal for truffles. Woodland clothes the steep slopes which rise from the valley floor — poplar and oak, chestnut, acacia. On the lower slopes, small fields are rimmed with scraps of woodland.

The visitors have parked several kilometres out of the town on both sides of the road, preferring to walk rather wait. I, too, park and walk. The bright autumn sun casts long shadows. There's a crisp bite to the air, whetting the appetite for what lies ahead.

The town is honey coloured, topped by a cartoon fortress, wider at the middle than it is at the base, crenellated and exquisitely proportioned. The fragrance of the noble tuber drifts across the sparkling piazza — today, all swept and polished, and empty of idlers. A line of stalls runs along one side of the colonnade. Every piazza in territory that harbours the truffle, a lover of damp, is colonnaded against the rain. Each stall has its guardian and its little piles of ivory nuggets carefully labelled with weight and price — which, inevitably, is twice as much as you'd expect. To the front of the stalls, a draw for the casual buyer and the tourists who might be induced to part with a handful of euros, are little piles of ivory pebbles laid on clean sheets of paper, clearly marked with value and weight. In the centre, proudly displayed in a little glass cabinet like Persian miniatures, the largest and most perfect ivory globes await the more serious

The huge choice of truffle-flavoured salami — salt-cured pork products being a local speciality in Le Marche — threatens to overwhelm the vendors.

purchaser. And for those without enough money even for these, there are dark-skinned, pale-fleshed summer truffles at a tenth of the price.

The lower parts of the town are crowded with families and groups of friends — all Italian, few tourists making their way this far inland — all on their Sunday outing and in their Sunday best. The car park, which doubles as the weekly market-place, is dense with food stalls — tented kiosks offering a peripatetic banquet — remarkably well-organized. Those who wish to take a seat at the long tables in the municipality's tent can buy a ticket for food at the entrance and exchange it for a truffled plateful at one of the cook-shops which line the rear. Prices are modest: a *piato misto* — three slices of truffled-topped crostini — is priced at 5.50 euros. For an extra euro, you may take your pick of the regional classics showered with truffles — black or white, everyday dishes are made special by the addition: *fonduta tartufata, crema di fagioli al Pecorino, trifolata de Pecorino, pasta con salsa tartufata.* Children and parents, friends and grandparents sip wine and chatter and chew. Over the loudspeakers, "Sweet Home Alabama" plays loudly on a loop.

The fair is still in full swing as the sun goes down. The cheese stalls have Parmesan and Pecorino and fat white curd-cheeses crusted with herbs. Piled

in a barrel are more cheeses the size of watermelons, matured in wine with deep red crusts. For those with a sweet tooth there are sticky Sicilian cakes, chocolate flavoured with chilli, marzipan fruits with rosy cheeks and painted freckles. The fast-food stall with the longest queue advertises its wares as *tortelli sulla lastra* — dough-turnovers cooked on the griddle — fist-sized envelopes filled with truffled potato, rolled thin as oatcakes and cut with a scalloped edge, like ravioli. Since this is chestnut territory, there is *castanaccio* — chestnut-flour flatbread flavoured with rosemary. Roasted chestnuts share space with freshly roasted corn-cobs — easy to eat since the stalks are left as handles. Next door has frying vats for *piada e piadina*: fine-rolled sheets of dough, deep-fried, puffed and golden and crisp, sold wrapped in sugar-paper, filled with a slice of prosciutto and, for those with the money, a shaving of truffle. For those who don't minding standing up at the bar, there are *lumache* — snails — in tomato sauce, and *rana fritte* — deep-fried frog's legs — to be washed down with rough red wine.

Truffled everything. Truffle butter, truffle vinegar, truffles and mushrooms, and truffled sauce, to name just those immediately visible.

On the vegetable stalls are neat ropes of garlic, dried red peppers and chillis on strings. There are all shapes and colours of onion, some plaited, some bunched: red, yellow, purple, ivory, pearl. There are, too, the usual smooth-tongued salesmen selling truffle-oaks in little pots, truffled honeys, truffled cheeses, even truffled grappa. For the children, there are cookie-stalls and cake-stalls selling winter fruits — oranges and lemons, melons, quinces and pomegranates, melons, medlars and *giuggiole*, shiny red-brown fruits that look like dates and taste like apples. And everywhere, drifting through the streets and round the castle walls, that inescapable fragrance: the scent of truffle.

A BLACK AND WHITE EXPERIENCE

While the truffles on offer in Sant'Agata — and in any market-square in the season in truffle territory — are the lesser end of the crop, the best, the most perfect, go to the wholesalers, who sell them to the packers: exporters who have access to foreign markets. Among these, Urbani is the name that counts. The firm's headquarters are in the hills above Spoleto, in the region of Norcia in Umbria, truffle territory which, unusually for Italy, has good supplies of the black and not much of the white.

Umbrian black and Piedmont white, rivals for more than a century, were joined together when Spoleto's Urbani outfit took over Alba's Morra — and when they did so, assumed control of more than half of the world's trade in both white and black truffles. Urbani nevertheless remains a family business, with, as is common in Italy, three generations working together. Although grandad Paolo is still the head of the enterprise, it's his daughter, Olga, and her two nephews who oversee the day-to-day running of what is surely one of the most profitable businesses in all Italy. The headquarters, a gleaming industrial temple — factory would be too inelegant a word — have been sited high in the hills, their isolation a discouragement to thieves; a dual-carriageway leads directly to the motorways and airports, essential for a business for which a few hours' delay can mean the loss of all profits.

Olga Urbani herself — willow-slender, exquisitely coiffed, chic as only a merchant princess can be — comes to the reception desk to greet us, her two visitors of the day. I am a newcomer, but Nancy Jenkins, my guide in the region, is an old friend and greeted with unmistakeable warmth. We are, however, in a rush. No time for a leisurely lunch, Olga explains regretfully. No time, in fact, for anything except "*magnato*", 100 kilos (220lbs) of which have just arrived from the company's buyer in Croatia. All must be sorted, graded, brushed and dispached within the day.

In Bosnia and Croatia, Olga explains, as we hurry down the corridor, both the Piedmont white and the Périgord black are found in abundance, though the whole crop goes for export. Perhaps this is because eating truffles is a declaration of status – a dilemma even when times are easy, which they rarely are in the Balkans. And if the truffle has no commercial value in its own territory, the hunter must look elsewhere. Croatia, with a population largely of German origin, exports much of its truffle harvest to Germany. The best comes to Italy, and the quality is good. The truth, it must be said, is that the largest truffle ever recorded was a "*magnato*" found in the Croatian province of Istria, in 1999, by Giancarlo Zigante – the biggest name in Balkan truffles – while scouring the woods with his dog, Diana. At the moment of lifting from its bed, witnesses confirmed that the tuber weighed nearly a kilo and a half (over three pounds) Wisely for his reputation – nothing is less believable than a man describing the size and perfection of a truffle he's already eaten – Zigante had the fungi's bulk cast in bronze before serving it to a hundred guests at a promotional banquet in the village where he found it. Other truffles gathered in the area – the Périgord black, the Burgundy and the summer truffle – have lately found their way to London. "Of course we didn't eat them ourselves," admitted the pretty young woman in charge of press relations at the launch for the company's products in Britain. "Actually, we had no idea this was even possible – but when we discovered we could sell them, that was a different matter."

As director of production, Olga is anxious to inspect the delivery herself. "You pay for a kilo, and three hours later it's down to nine hundred grams, so you understand we have to work quickly."

We hurry down the corridor. The sorting room, protected by thick steel doors that swing open at a touch, is a steel-lined vault, white-tiled, temperature-controlled – an operating theatre just waiting for the surgeon. In spite of the chill, the fragrance is everywhere, overwhelming the senses, dizzying – as if the huge white space is filled with the essence of truffle, the

"Melano" or "magnato"? The white truffle (or "magnato" opposite, left) and the black truffle (or "melano" opposite, right); each has its advocates.

concentrated fragrance of every truffle every born. The day's delivery — ivory-coloured rocks heaped in baskets — is the source of the astonishing scent. This is the moment of maximum vulnerability, says Olga, pulling out truffles at random. When a delivery arrives, at least one member of the Urbani family is always in the white-tiled sorting room, keeping track. The surveillance cameras in the ceiling are there to prevent misunderstandings, says Olga. They avoid confusion. And since even a perfectly ordinary truffle is worth as much as a labourer can earn in a day, temptation is real.

Olga's nephew, Carlo, is in charge today. Those truffles not of the first quality are set aside for use in peripheral products — the truffled pastes and creams with which the company pays most of its wages. Those that remain are good enough for the chefs. These perfect nuggets are brushed, rinsed and rolled in a fine coating of golden dust. "Odd, I know," says Olga. "But the chefs like it and the customers expect it." The truffles are nestled one by one in their woven wicker boxes lined with checkered cloth, a kilo (over two pounds) apiece, 20 per box. "Good marketing starts with the packaging," says Olga. "The chefs can set the box on a table for the clients to see when they come through the door. If they want to know, they can ask the price — but most people don't. People know they're expensive. That's part of the magic.

But you must judge for yourself. Since I cannot offer you lunch, we'll make sure you remember your dinner."

Olga is as good as her word. Heaven only knows whether it was the truffles we were carrying or simply the excitement of the day itself, but the journey home took twice as long as the journey out. Anyone who has ever shared a confined space with even a single modest little truffle, let alone a whole kilo of Urbani's finest, will recognize the problem. The fragrance — or whatever it is which raises emotional temperatures — has a way of causing perfectly rational beings, pigs and so forth, to behave quite out of character. The effect, in my own experience, is to quicken the pulse while softening the brain, a process not unfamiliar to some of us which leads, when experienced in the right company. . . but let it pass.

That evening, bidden to dinner elsewhere, we take the decision to share. Our hostess, an American writer resident in Paris — drawn to Europe in the 1970s for its intellectual freedoms — had bought the house before Tuscany became fashionable among expatriots. The house, stone-built, lacking mains water and electricity, has been preserved much as the previous owners, independent *contadini*, had left it. Subsequently, she had fallen into the habit of inviting friends to help her crop the olive-trees that came with the purchase. Among visitors over the years was Germaine Greer, who wrote a book on her experience of unfettered love among the Tuscans. Ms Greer's view was balanced, some years later, by Frances Mayes' romantic account of the good life in the region, drawing a new audience of enthusiasts to take up residence in the area.

Most of us at the dinner are no longer in the market for romantic engagements — whether spoken-for or beyond such entertainments — but not all. One of our number, pale face half-hidden by a curtain of curls, removes her spectacles. The brightness of the candlelight reveals violet eyes, full lips and the alabaster skin of — well — youth and beauty. The revelation has an electric effect on one of our number, a Japanese sculptor dressed like a Samurai, thickset, pony-tailed, old enough to know better, whose fierce expression and broken Italian had, up until that moment, made communication impossible. Not now.

"*Per amore Dio!*" he shouts. "*E jovene!*"

His need to point out that one among us is somewhat younger than the rest startles our hostess. Glancing between "youth-and-beauty" and her not-so-young admirer, she takes a deep breath. "I see," she says, and smiles. Then, more thoughtfully, "We were told there were truffles to be dug from the terrace. Perhaps we should check. And then again. . . " with a sidelong glance, "perhaps not."

A clatter of plates announces the risotto.

"You brought the truffle, Lisabetta," says our hostess. "Do the honours." Without further instruction she hands me the slicer. I hesitate — of course I do. The apportioning of a truffle is a grave responsibility. Our hostess will have none of it. I cannot refuse. Grasping the truffle in one hand and the slicer in the other, I work my way round the table. It's strangely pleasurable, this showering of steaming rice with shards of fragrant fungus.

Dreamily, I am about to embark on another round when my wrist is gripped and both truffle and grater are eased from my fingers.

"Stop!" The voice is agonized. "I have to tell you, I cannot help it!" My assailant gently cups my face in his hands and plants a whiskery kiss on my cheek. "I am Italian, from Milano. I must speak." Another whiskery consolation. "You cut it too thick. I know that you mean to be generous, but it's not how it's done. For the white truffle, the cut must be fine, the flesh must always be transparent. The black — well, you may cut it any way you please. Are we agreed? Of course we are. Next time you'll know."

Everyone relaxes. Most of us are Italian — everyone understands. Talk turns to the effect of the truffle on those who share it. It's possible, everyone agrees, that the truffle creates an atmosphere. Opinions divide on whether or not it's seductive. It's certainly delicious, declares our hostess, but can it actually be said to be aphrodisiac? Is there proof? Could it be that it only worked for the converted? For those who were already in love? And what about friends, unconnected by yearnings of the sort said to be encouraged by the fragrance? Could it turn friends into lovers, however briefly?

"Indeed it can," says "youth-and-beauty" suddenly. "And I shall tell you how? I was among friends, just as we are tonight. We had arranged to eat together in a restaurant at a time of year when, just as now, there were truffles. We ordered, as the menu advised, a plate of *fettucini tartufati*, creamy and perfect, to share between us. The scent was wonderful, lingering. I could smell it on my breath for days.

"But that is not the point of my story. There was a man among us, a friend I'd known for years. There was never anything between us. I'd never been interested, never even found him particularly attractive. But then suddenly, in the middle of the meal when our mouths were full of truffle, he leaned over and kissed me — a long truffle-fragrant kiss, the kind that lovers exchange. It was unimaginably exquisite. I didn't even protest. And then he stopped. And it was over. We continued the conversation as if nothing had happened. And truly nothing happened before or later. But I've never forgotten it. And sometimes, when we meet again as friends, I wonder if he remembers what we did."

"*Certo*. Of course he does," says the sculptor, moving towards her purposefully. Lowering his head to hers, he kisses her on the lips. "Like this?"

She considers the question thoughtfully, then shakes her head. "No." Then adds by way of explanation, "There was a great deal more tongue."

And, with that brutal dismissal, "youth-and-beauty" replaces her glasses, pony-tail returns to his corner and the talk turns, as it often does when truffles scent the air, to tales of other amorous encounters experienced in similar situations — memories that have not lasted in my head, since none was as startling as the first admission, and none was accompanied by the fragrance that makes such stories memorable.

Later, tucked up in my bed in a truffle-induced stupor with only an ancient copper hot-water bottle for company, I mull over the events of the evening. Particularly, it must be said, my own shortcomings in the matter of truffle grating.

No question that my chastiser was right.

There's a difference, too, between the white and the black in the way the fragrance is delivered. While the black is best appreciated by the tongue and teeth, the white is for the nose and the throat: having made its mark, it lingers longer. The perfume is perceived as soon as knife blade parts flesh, and in direct proportion to the surface exposed to air. That's to say, the thinner the sliver, the more bang you get for the buck. Money for money, two thin slices pack twice the punch of one thick. My instructor was right to be offended — I had squandered a treasure. Secure in the warmth of my bed, I told myself I'd never make the same mistake again. And then I thought, perversely, perhaps I will. A feast is not a feast unless there's waste. If Cleopatra drank pearls dissolved in wine, and Caesar ate roasted peacocks with gilded crests — why should the rest of us not eat too much truffle?

The dealers take time to confer at the Mercato del Tartufo in Alba before business gets into full swing.

ALBA'S TRUFFLES

The traditional centre of the truffle trade is Alba, a turreted medieval town set among the vineyards of the valley of the Tanaro River in Piedmont, the province which borders Provence, took a lead from Napoléon Bonaparte, and provided Italy, though briefly, with her unifying monarchy. Alba's truffle festival — the Fiera Nazionale del Tartufo Bianco — is the most famous in all Italy and runs for three weeks in September, and afterwards every Saturday until the end of December. The *fiera* takes place in the elegant Piazza Maddalena and continues along the Via Maestra and the Via Vittorio Emanuele, under the arcade. In Asti, the next most important of Piedmont's truffle towns, the action is to be found in the Caffé San Carlo, Via Cavour.

Throughout the region, the name of note is Giacomo Morra, Alba's truffle-godfather and controller of the Piedmont trade till he sold out to Urbani. Morra was above all a showman, a man who understood the value of spin. It was Morra who set up the truffle festa which runs every year in Alba and has been copied, with varying degrees of success, in every truffle town in Italy. He, too, it

was who took the decision to present the best of the crop to a personality-of-the-year of his choice. These choices were engagingly personal: the first, soon after the end of World War II, was President Eisenhower; Hollywood was represented by Alfred Hitchcock as well as Marilyn Monroe; Brigitte Bardot was balanced by the Pope. As the market expanded, this tactic — maximum publicity for minimum expenditure — developed into the charity truffle auctions which hit the headlines at the start of every season, setting absurdly high prices for a crop which immediately, by comparison, becomes a bargain — leading one to suppose the secret's all in the presentation.

Not so. Snake-oil salesmanship may have something to do with it, but it's not the real story, as food-and-travel writer William Black discovered on a visit to Alba a few years ago in fiera time. At first sight, contrary to his expectations and in spite of congenial female company, he found the atmosphere surprisingly decorous: "the *fiera*. . . was rather elegant and courteous, with truffles sitting

Left: A quiet moment in the Piazza Maddalena before opening hours.
Below: Small glass domes protect truffles from evaporation as well as from prying fingers.

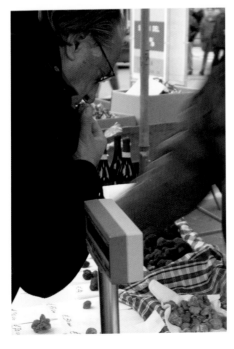

respectfully under glass on sheets of rice paper. The only slight hint of vulgarity is the price, which at times will make you laugh."

As soon as the glass is removed and the fragrance liberated, the picture's different: "There in your hand sits this magical minuscule moon, pitted with craters, utterly mysterious. . . is there something deeply and atavistically sexual about its perfume? Truffles," he muses, "smell for a reason."

Of course they do. But there's a discernible difference between the black and the white in the way it can be appreciated. While the black truffle is robust in both texture and fragrance — offering resistance to the teeth as well as a smoothness and silkiness to the tongue, the white is fragile, ethereal in texture as well as fragrance. When prepared with delicacy, its flesh has a translucent silkiness, a supple paperiness like dampened parchment, or the just discarded skin of a snake. This impression of fragility is heightened by the fine pattern of veining, like the crumpled wings of a newly hatched butterfly, visible when the ribbons fall on something warm. To test the truth of this, pile your plate high and crown it with a thick blanket of truffle ribbons. Then lower your head towards the dish and breathe deeply, drawing the scent first into your lungs and then, by holding your breath as if inhaling halucinogenic smoke, absorb the fragrance into the bloodstream.

The truffle is for adults and innocents — grown-ups who recognize it and babies who have not yet learned to distrust it, though it's not, in my experience, a scent that appeals to their older siblings. Offer it just the same, and when they wrinkle their little noses and refuse to touch it, tell them no matter, this is for memory's sake. They'll know it again when the time is ripe.

Clockwise from top left: truffled cheeses; porcini, which share the same truffle territory; truffle-flavoured salami with other artisan pork products; "magnato" fresh from the earth – the nose knows. Overleaf: Fresh or not? The truth is in the fragrance, as this Italian dealer demonstrates.

ITALIAN WHITE TRUFFLE RECIPES

RISOTTO AL VINO ROSSO TARTUFATO
Risotto with red wine and truffles

In Piedmont, truffle dishes are paired with Barolo, the wine of the territory — as they say in the dialect: *bun pi bun fa bun*, "good with good makes twice as good" — here used as the cooking liquid. For extra creaminess, Italian chefs prefer *carnaroli* or *vialone nano* to arborio for a risotto. Out of season, stir the rice just before serving with a teaspoon of truffle butter or paste, or fragranced oil, and top with flakes of Parmesan.

SERVES 4

600ml (1¼ pints) red wine
600ml (1¼ pints) chicken stock
1 tablespoon unsalted butter
1 tablespoon extra virgin olive oil
2 tablespoons finely chopped red onion
350g (12oz) risotto rice
Sea salt and freshly ground black pepper
85g (3oz) freshly grated Parmesan

TO FINISH
1 fresh white truffle (30-50g/1-2 oz), cleaned

Warm the wine in a pan to just below simmering point. In another pan, heat the stock. Have these ready to add to the rice.

In a heavy risotto-pan, melt the butter gently with the olive oil. Add the onion and cook until soft — don't let it brown. Add the rice and raise the heat a little. Cook, stirring, till the rice is translucent. Add a ladleful of the warm wine and raise the heat a little. Cook, stirring, until the wine has been absorbed. Lower the heat a little and add more wine. Continue until all has been absorbed. Don't let the rice dry out completely between additions. Add the stock in the same way till the rice is tender but still a little resistant at the centre — you may not need it all.

Remove from the heat, stir in 2 tablespoons of the grated Parmesan, taste and add salt and pepper. Cover and set aside to rest for 5-7 minutes. Serve in deep plates, handing the truffle and its grater separately.

TAGLIATELLE AL SUGO CON TARTUFI
Tagliatelle with tomato sauce and truffles

In Umbria, they think nothing of combining their truffles with a robust ham-flavoured *sugo*, a habit deplored in Piedmont. The region also makes very fine pork products, including an elegant prosciutto and a first-class mortadella. If you'd like to make your own tagliatelle, for a whole-egg pasta, you need 10 eggs to a kilo (2lb) of flour. Failing fresh truffles, stir in a tablespoon of truffle paste and finish with fine flakes of Parmesan.

SERVES 4

250g (½lb) dried or 500g (1lb) fresh tagliatelle

SUGO

1 small onion, chopped

2-3 garlic cloves, chopped

2 tablespoons olive oil

1 tablespoon finely diced prosciutto

About 1kg (2lb) tomatoes, skinned, de-seeded and chopped (or 1 large can)

1 small glass red wine

Small sprig rosemary

1 tablespoon grated Parmesan

TO FINISH

1 fresh white truffle (30-50g/1-2oz), cleaned

Prepare the *sugo* first. Fry the onion and garlic gently in the oil in a large pan until they soften – don't let them take colour. Add the chopped prosciutto, tomatoes, red wine and rosemary, allow to bubble up and then mash down to encourage the tomato flesh to collapse. Leave to simmer very gentle for 30-40 minutes, till thick and rich.

Bring a large saucepan of water to the boil, add a teaspoon of salt, and drop in the pasta. Turn up the heat (don't cover the saucepan) and bring everything back to the boil. If using fresh pasta, allow one big belch and drain; if dried, cook for 6-8 minutes (check instructions on the packet). Don't drain it too thoroughly. Transfer the pasta to a warm bowl into which you have poured a little olive oil, add a ladleful of the *sugo* and toss to coat the pasta. Serve the pasta on hot plates (speed is very important) and hand the rest of the *sugo* separately along with the truffle and its grater, much as you would a hunk of Parmesan.

UOVO AL BURRO CON TARTUFO
Eggs fried in butter with truffle

The simplest way with a fresh Piedmont truffle, this dish is the one most frequently recommended by those who gather their own. The only possible substitute for fresh is a flash-frozen truffle — don't defrost it first, just allow it 5 minutes in the warmth of the kitchen and grate it straight onto the hot egg.

SERVES 1

2 perfectly fresh free-range eggs
50g (2oz) unsalted butter
1 fresh white truffle (25-30g/1-1¼oz), cleaned

TO SERVE
Unsalted Tuscan bread (or any sourdough bread)
Sea salt

Allow the eggs to come up to room temperature. Melt the butter in a small frying pan. As soon as it foams but before it browns, crack in the eggs. Fry till the white is set and the yolk is still runny. Transfer to a hot plate and shower with grated truffle. You'll need thick-cut white bread and sea salt on the side.

LASAGNE INCASSETTATA TARTUFFATO
Baked lasagne with truffles

A robust baked pasta dish, from the Marche, which includes a background flavouring of the summer black truffle in the sauce while the white provides the finishing fragrance. If fresh truffle is unobtainable, use a teaspoon of truffle paste in the sauce and replace the white with shavings of Parmesan.

SERVES 4

250g (8oz) green lasagne (dried)
1 tablespoons olive oil
1 black summer truffle (about 50g/2oz)
2 level tablespoons unsalted butter
2 level tablespoons plain flour
4 tablespoons diced prosciutto
600ml (1¼ pints) full-cream milk
Salt and pepper

TO FINISH
4 tablespoons mascarpone (or full-fat cream cheese)
4 tablespoons grated Parmesan or Pecorino cheese
1 egg, well-whisked

TO SERVE
1 fresh white truffle (30-50g/1-2oz), cleaned

Cook the lasagne in plenty of boiling salted water with the oil until tender but still firm – 6-7 minutes – passing it through cold water as you drain it, leaving it a little wet so the sheets don't stick together.

Meanwhile, clean the truffle carefully and dice it, including the black exterior – this is a country dish, nothing dainty. Melt the butter in a heavy saucepan and stir in the flour. Fry gently, stirring, till the mixture looks sandy. Toss in the diced ham and truffle, and let it feel the heat for a moment. Add the milk or cream, allow to bubble up and stir until smooth and thick enough to coat the back of a wooden spoon – about 5 minutes.

Fold the mascarpone with the grated cheese (saving a spoonful for finishing) and the well-whisked egg.

Preheat the oven to 180C/350F/Gas mark 4.

Lightly oil the base of a medium-sized gratin dish and line with a layer of lasagne (you'll need about a third of it). Spread with half the truffle sauce and top with another layer of lasagne. Repeat the layering. Top with the mascarpone mixture and sprinkle with the reserved grated cheese. Bake for 10-15 minutes, till brown and bubbling. Shower with finely grated ribbons of white truffle just before serving.

POLENTA CON CAVALO E TARTUFO
Polenta with cabbage and truffle

A robust polenta dish from the Langhe, made in the old days with chestnut flour. Failing fresh truffles, flash-frozen will do, particularly if you include a little truffle butter.

SERVES 4-6

500g (1lb) fine-ground cornmeal
50g (2oz) butter
About 250g (½lb) finely-shredded, dark green cabbage
Sea salt

TO FINISH
1 fresh white truffle (about 30-50g/1-2oz), cleaned
50g (2oz) Parmesan

Mix half the cornmeal with 250ml (½ pint) cold water until smooth and free of lumps. Bring 2 litres (3 pints) water to the boil in a heavy pan with the butter and a level teaspoon of salt. Stir in the watered cornmeal and bring to the boil. Add the cabbage. Cook for about 10 minutes, until the cabbage is tender. Sprinkle in the rest of the cornmeal, bring back the boil and stir over the heat for another 20-30 minutes (depending on the fineness of the grind), until the mixture is thick and pulls away from the base of the pan; if you need extra water, make sure it's boiling. Heap in a warm bowl and finish at the table with fine shavings of truffle and Parmesan.

TAJARIN SIENESE
Taglionini with cream and truffles

A fresh egg-yolk pasta, very rich and delicate, dressed with a cream and wine sauce and topped with fine ribbons of white truffle. If you don't want to make your own pasta, you'll need 500g (1lb) fresh or 350g (12oz) dried all-egg tagliatelle — the yellower the better. Or combine the sauce with a pasta aromatized with truffle and finish with finely sliced button mushrooms sprinkled with a little truffle oil — not the real thing, but good enough to convey the general idea.

SERVES 4

THE PASTA
350g (12 oz) grano flour (double-zero, for preference)
4 large egg yolks
1 tablespoon olive oil
Salt

THE SAUCE
50g (2oz) butter
4 tablespoons white wine
150ml (¼pt) fresh cream or mascarpone
Pinch grated nutmeg
Freshly ground pepper
50g (2oz) freshly grated Parmesan

TO FINISH
1 fresh white truffle (about 50g/2oz), cleaned

Make the pasta first. Heap the flour onto your work-surface or a well-scrubbed kitchen table, mix in the salt, make a dip in the flour with your fist and drop in the egg-yolks and a tablespoon of olive oil. Work the dry ingredients into the wet, drawing the flour into the yolks with your fingers until you have a sticky paste — you will probably need a tablespoon or two of water. Knead with the heel of your hand and your fist — punching and pummelling — until the dough is thoroughly elastic and smooth. Wrap in clingfilm and leave in a cool place for half an hour to rest. Roll out the dough as thinly as possible — cut the dough into two pieces to make it easier to manage — or use a pasta roller. Either roll up the sheet of dough like a little carpet and cut into very thin ribbons, or cut on the narrowest gauge of the pasta-roller's cutters. Toss the pasta ribbons lightly with your fingers to separate the strands and leave to dry and firm a little — 30 minutes or so.

Bring a large pan of water to the boil and salt it generously. Pasta needs plenty of water. Set a roomy serving bowl to warm. Meanwhile make the sauce: melt the butter gently in a small pan, add the wine, allow to bubble up until the alcohol has evaporated and the liquid reduced by half, then stir in the cream or mascarpone, reheat till boiling, season with nutmeg and freshly ground pepper, stir in the Parmesan, then taste and add salt.

Call all participants to table. Drop the pasta lightly into the boiling water, return the pan to the boil as quickly as possible (which is why you start with plenty of water), give it a quick stir to separate the strands, count to 20 and transfer to a colander — fresh pasta needs no more than 30 seconds in all. Don't drain it too thoroughly but leave it a little damp. Tip the pasta into the warm bowl and toss with the sauce.

Serve piled on hot plates. Blanket each serving with fine gratings of white truffle. That's all.

BAGNA CAUDA AL TARTUFO
Olive oil and anchovy with truffles

The perfect way to serve a Piedmont truffle fresh from its bed: a warm bath
of olive oil flavoured with anchovies, melted together to form a pungent little
dipping sauce. If no fresh truffles are available, add a drop of truffle oil to the
dip and serve with crunchy raw vegetables — fine slivers of raw baby artichoke,
green asparagus, baby turnips.

SERVES 4-6 AS AN ANTIPASTO

1 small can salt-cured anchovies (6-8 fillets)
2-3 cloves garlic, skinned
2 slices dry bread
1 tablespoon white wine
1 litre (2 scant pints) mild extra-virgin olive oil

TO SERVE
Day-old sourdough bread, chunked into bite-sized pieces
Sea salt
White truffles — 75g (3oz), or as much as you can afford, cleaned

OPTIONAL EXTRAS
1-2 fennel bulbs, washed and separated into bite-sized segments
1 head celery, washed and cut into short lengths

You'll need a saucepan and spirit-lamp arrangement to keep the oily sauce
warm on the table. The Italians can buy a neat little earthenware casserole
with its own built-in holder, though a fondue set will do fine.

Drain the anchovies. If you've bought them loose from a barrel (as in Italy)
they'll need a preliminary soaking in milk to get rid of excess salt — 30
minutes will do. Crumble the bread and put it to soak in the wine for a few
minutes, then squeeze out excess liquid using your fist. Crush the garlic with
the salt — use a food processor or pestle and mortar — add the anchovies and
the bread, and pound all to a paste. Transfer the paste to whatever casserole
or pan you've chosen to bring it to table, stir in the oil and heat gently until
all is well mixed. Remove just before it bubbles.

Provide each participant with a plate, a large napkin and a long-handled fork. Set the pan on the table and keep it warm. Everyone dips their bread into the salty oil and eats it with a topping of grated truffle. Serve the optional fennel or celery to refresh the palate between bites.

RISO ALLA PIEMONTESE
Baked rice with truffle

A venerable risotto in which the grains are not subjected to the usual preliminary turning in hot oil or butter, but are plainly cooked in chicken stock and finished in the oven. I have adapted the recipe from a cookbook published in the 1880s by Giovanni Vialardi, chef to Vittorio Emanuele, Italy's first monarch.

SERVES 4-6

500g (1 lb) risotto rice (arborio, roma or carnaroli)
About 1 litre (1½ pints) chicken stock
Salt and freshly ground pepper

TO FINISH
1 fresh white truffle (30-50g/1-2oz), cleaned
50g (2oz) unsalted butter
50g (2oz) freshly grated Parmesan

Preheat the oven to 180C/350F/Gas mark 4.

Meanwhile, wash, drain and measure the volume of the rice. Measure out twice the volume of stock to rice. Bring the measured stock to the boil in a large pot, stir in the rice, return to the boil and transfer to an ovenproof casserole. Cover and bake for 30-40 minutes, till the broth has all been absorbed and the rice is tender.

Stir half the butter and half the Parmesan into the rice. Remove half the rice and reserve, top the remaining rice with a layer of finely grated truffle, replace the reserved rice, dot with small scraps of the remaining butter and the rest of the Parmesan and bake for another 10 minutes or so, till a light crust has formed.

FONDUTA CON TARTUFI
Cheese fondue with truffles

If you can lay your hands on a fresh *"magnato"*, ask three of your best friends to share the feast — as with a pound of caviar, four is the maximum number to one good-sized truffle. If necessary, you can replace the Fontina with half Gruyère and half Emmenthal cheese.

SERVES 4

300g (10oz) Fontina cheese
300ml (½ pint) single cream
4 egg yolks

TO FINISH
1 good-sized (30-50g/1-2oz) fresh white truffle, cleaned

TO SERVE
Toasted country bread or plain-cooked potatoes, boiled or baked
Unsalted butter

Chop the cheese into tiny pieces with a sharp knife — worth the effort since it produces a smoother mix than if you grate it, but a food processor will do the job in no time.

Put the cheese into a basin with the milk warmed to blood heat. Stand the basin over a saucepanful of boiling water. Cover it with a clean cloth. The milk and cheese must be kept warm on the side of the stove for an hour, so that the cheese melts very gently into the milk.

While you are waiting, make a plain risotto, or prepare thick slices of fresh bread for each of your guests. Put four plates to warm.

At the end of the hour whisk the egg yolks with the cheese and milk. Put the saucepan on the heat and bring its water to the boil. Turn it down to simmer. Carry on whisking while the mixture thickens over the simmering water. Don't hurry it. When the mixture has thickened so that it can comfortably blanket the back of a wooden spoon, take it off the heat.

Make sure your friends are all at table, each with a warm plate on which you have placed either a thick slice of bread scattered with little pieces of fresh butter or a mound of risotto.

Pour the fonduta over the bread or potatoes — or hand the pan to participants and let them serve themselves — along with the truffle and its grater.

CARNE ALL'ALBESE
Carpaccio with truffles

A refinement of the classic Piedmont raw-steak preparation — basically, a steak tartare dressed with oil and lemon and topped with white truffle. This is the version served in Luigi Ciciriello's truffle-brasserie in Brussels as a quick counter-snack, simple and perfect. If fresh truffle is not available, add a teaspoon of truffle oil and a knifetip of crushed garlic to the lemon-oil dressing, and finish with flakes of Parmesan.

SERVES 2

150g (6oz) fillet of veal or young beef in a single piece
2 leaves escarole or frisée chicory
2 sticks celery, finely sliced

TO DRESS
4 tablespoons extra virgin olive oil
1 tablespoon lemon juice
A little sea salt
Freshly milled pepper

TO FINISH
1 small white truffle (30g/1oz), cleaned

Wrap the meat in cling-film and pop it in the freezer for an hour or two until frozen solid.

Arrange the lettuce, separated into small pieces, on a serving dish. Slice the frozen meat with a sharp knife as finely as possible. Place the slices between two sheets of clingfilm and press hard with a rolling pin to flatten.

Sprinkle the lettuce with fine slices of celery and cover with the meat. Dress with oil, lemon juice, salt and pepper and top with finely sliced truffle.

Truffles around the World

While there are literally hundreds of truffle species in every corner of the globe, most of them are too small or too unpalatable to be of any use to the cook. Those which are large and fragrant enough to be of gastronomic interest have been gathered, say experts, for around 4,000 years.

Most notable of the newcomers is the Oregon truffle, an American native mostly symbiotic on pine, while the most contentious is the Chinese black, *Tuber sinensis*, a "*melano*" look-alike, which has recently been causing consternation in both France and Italy. Of Old World varieties, *T. aestivum* (also known as *T. albidum*), the summer black — the only truffle of note in Britain — is esteemed in Italy and France as a background-flavouring to the Piedmont white and the Périgord black, as well as its more obvious value as a make-weight for the labelling in commercially prepared truffle-pastes and truffle-butters. The botanical outsiders, since most, though not all, belong to the *Terfezia* species, are the desert truffles; these, though they rarely come on the market outside their own areas, are esteemed in their own territories, though they're treated rather more casually — sold, cooked and eaten much as other roots such as potatoes — since the fragrance is far less discernible. No doubt there are other truffles, equally exquisite, waiting to be discovered in other places. For the moment, however, we must make the best of what we have.

Small but precious. The Oregon truffle is highly prized in North America, and its popularity is increasing rapidly.

ENGLISH AND BURGUNDY TRUFFLES

The only palatable truffles found in England (or the rest of the UK) are the summer truffles (*T.aestivum* or *T. albidum*). They are also known, I'm told by those who like to be precise, as the red-grained black truffle. In Italy these truffles are commonly known as *scorzone*, in France as *truffes d'été* or *truffes de St Jean* (since they comes to maturity around midsummer). No doubt in recognition of its popularity on the other side of the Channel, it is also known as the *truffe anglaise*. The most widespread of all the valued truffles, it is to be found also in Scandinavia, Germany, throughout the Iberian Peninsula, through Central and Eastern Europe as far as the steppes of Russia, across Mongolia and into China, where its given name is *xia kuai jun*. In the hand, the *peridium* is black with reddish tints, the *glebum* is ivory to dark brown with veining. The season lasts from May to November.

In Britain, John Evelyn, writing in *Acetaria*, a gardening manual with recipes, published in 1699, describes the finding of truffles in Northamptonshire: "[A friend] had gleaned from a letter that appeared in the Philosophical Transactions of the Royal Society that truffles had been found on English soil,and a great fungus hunt had sent gatherers scratching and rooting all over England for these subterranean gems." In modern times, food-witer Jane Grigson says the last of the truffle hunters in England, Alfred Collins of Winterslow in Wiltshire, gave up in 1935. When, some twenty or so years ago, the *Observer* ran a truffle-finding competition, enormous quantities were unearthed throughout the land, most, as it happened, from the Scottish borders where they were, it was thought, symbiotic on Caledonian pine.

While in the south and east of Britain, much of the truffle's natural habitat has been lost to the woodman's axe, there are still plenty to be found in the woodlands and new plantings by those who know where and when to look. Naturally I cannot, on pain of never being permitted a return visit, give the location of one of the most prolific hauls ever recorded in Britain. Enough to say that the plantation of young beech trees on which the crop depends is on private land so close to the thunderous roar of the M4 you can feel the vibrations in your toes. Since everything on the edge of a motorway is shaken towards the surface, truffles grown close to a busy road tend to sit high in their beds. The beeches on which the crop was discovered are no more than twelve years old. The trees, planted as a commercial crop for wood, are neatly spaced, with plenty of light and air between. The earth itself, at midsummer already cropped and under plough for a second crop, is chalk-white fading to ochre and burgundy.

The owners of the plantation were astonished by what they'd found: "At first we didn't really believe it, but we checked in the manual and sent some to Kew to do the chemistry, and there was no doubt. The price is nothing like the white or the black, but it's good money, just the same. We sell some, we eat some and we give some away."

An English truffle hunt must start from scratch. First, the terrain must be suitable – chalk is essential – and the host-trees must be present. Next it's a matter of selecting a likely tree. Sparse undergrowth and a slight balding of the moss and grass in a root-wide radius round the trunk is a good indicator. Then, on your knees, feel delicately under the surface layer of moss and leaf-debris – a little like an experienced seducer might rummage in his lady-love's underpinnings – till your hand encounters a firm lump. This will either be a compacted ball of grass roots, a stone, or, if luck is with you, a spherical tuber, uneven, rough to the touch, which may need to be carefully excavated and prised from its bed. The soil, being light, releases the tuber easily.

In the hand, the sphere is uneven, sometimes with several lobes, with a hard black outer-surface formed of small pyramid-shapes, firm and heavy for its size. The largest of the haul we found that day weighed more than pound, the smallest no more than half an ounce. There is no difference in perfume – a ripe small truffle is every bit as good as a monster. When cut, the surface is as smooth as silk, the colour of creamy coffee, with a delicate ivory veining. The scent, when newly released, is powerful, pheromone-laden, musky, flowery – if the nose did the judging, it could easily be mistaken for the Périgord black (*Tuber melanosporum*). But the perfume is more powerful than the flavour, which lacks the punch of the Périgord truffle. The texture in the mouth is velvety, firm, mealy when pressed between the teeth.

The English truffle's closest relative is *Tuber uncinatum,* the Burgundy truffle. Experts are divided on whether it's actually the same species – a late-ripening version of *T. aestivum.* Its likes and dislikes are identical. Its habitat is forest and woodland with well-spaced or broken tree-cover, when it takes advantage of every gap – rides, clearings, pathways, even spaces left by fallen trees. Undemanding of terrain, it thrives in the calcereous regions of central and eastern France and has also colonized Austria's pine-forests. Its adaptability is likely to make it of increasing economic importance, since it thrives in cultivation and is esteemed for its fragrance and texture in both France and Italy. In France, where experts maintain they can distinguish it from *T. aestivum* in the hand and on the nose, it's known as *truffe grise de Bourgogne*. It's in season from early October to the end of December.

A typical English woodland of a type favourable to truffles.

LESSER EUROPEAN TRUFFLES

These varieties — dozens in all — are those that are edible but lack the characteristics of the esteemed varieties or possess them in unpalatable form. They are usually present wherever the more valuable truffles are found, colonizing their habitats and confusing the unwary. The jury's still out on how much cross-breeding takes place, though it's certain that

they're perfectly capable of taking over a truffle plantation and contaminating the stock.

One of the most widespread of the lesser black varieties — gathered along the Atlantic seaboard from Finland to Portugal, throughout Central Europe and around the Mediterranean littoral as far as Turkey — is *Tuber brumale* (*T.moschatum*), the musk or violet truffle, known in France as *truffe musquée, truffe violette, truffe puante, truffle rougeotte* and *truffe vermande du Poitou* and in Italy as the stinking truffle (*tartufo fetido*) while in Turkey, somewhat confusingly, it's one of several varieties which go by the name of *keme*. Although it actually prefers a cooler climate and a richer, damper soil than "*melano*", since it's generally more tolerant of both host and terrain, it readily colonizes territory occupied by "*melano*", making itself thoroughly unwelcome among plantation owners. Other breeds of black truffle of minor gastronomic interest include *Tuber maculatum*, known in France as *truffe tâchetée*; *Tuber cibarium*, which is one of several varieties, including "*melano*" and *T. aestivum*, known in Spain as *criadillas de tierra* — earth testicles (well — they're dark, round and laden with pheromones) — and in Britain, somewhat less imaginatively, as the ordinary black truffle; and *T. mesentericum*, the mesenteric or Bagnoli truffle.

Several of the black truffles have a reddish tinge, though none more red than the dog-nosed truffle (*Tuber rufum* or *T. olivaceum*), found in Italy (where it's known as the *tartufo roso*), in France (known as *truffe rouge, truffe rougâtre, truffe nez de chien*), in Spain (as *trufa roja*) and in Portugal (as *trufa vermelha*). Where its territories overlap with the terfezia species, it's known in Arabic as *kam-ah hamra*.

Most notable of the lesser white truffles is *Tuber borchii* — known as *bianchetto* in Italy and *truffe blanchâtre* in France — which comes to maturity in January and might, at the beginning of the season (when they overlap for a week or two), be mistaken for the Piedmont white. A small-sized (rarely larger than a walnut), cream-coloured truffle, it has a pleasant, somewhat garlicky aroma. By April, the end of the season, when the fragrance is more distinct, it darkens to tan. The majority of the crop disappears into commercial truffle preparations — sauces and purées. Other pale varieties that might, to the untutored eye, be taken for "*magnato*" are *Tuber album*, one of several in Italy known as *tartufo bianco*; *Tuber exavatum*, known in France as the yellow truffle (*truffe jaune*); *Tuber gennadii* (or *T. lacunosum*), which is known in Italy as the ordinary *tartufo bianco*.

CHINESE TRUFFLES

In Asia there are truffles (*Tuber sinensis, T. himalayense, T. indicum*) that can all easily be mistaken for *Tuber melanosporum*, the Périgord black. Their colour is similar – chocolate to black with matching interior. The flavour and fragrance is very variable. Some have plenty of fragrance, others virtually none, but all will take the scent of the superior truffle if left in proximity overnight. *Tuber sinensis* can leave a bitter aftertaste, while all three can deliver a distinct whiff of petrol – though this is also true of over-the-hill European truffles, and is the reason why cheap artificial truffle-fragrances are petrol-derivatives. Olga Urbani describes the flesh of the oriental truffles as like chewing cork: "They have no scent, no perfume, no flavour, but if you drop them in a box of real truffles overnight, they'll take the scent." Other truffle fanciers are more enthusistic and will tell you it all depends on the batch, and the time out of the soil. Don't expect too much and never pay more than you'd usually expect to pay for any ordinary wild-gathered fungi. Use them in combinations of other mushrooms, wild or cultivated, much as you would the summer truffle, and you won't be disappointed. To the untutored eye it's very easy to mistake it for *Tuber melanosporum*.

NORTH AMERICAN TRUFFLES

Among North American native truffles found in the Pacific North-west, two are of particular gastronomic interest, the Oregon white (*Tuber gibbosum*), and the Oregon black (*Leucangium carthusiana*) – formerly *Picoa carthusiana* in an earlier classification, of which the former is the more highly esteemed. Interest in North American truffles among chefs and gourmets is of relatively recent date and can be ascribed, initially at least, to the enthusiasm of the godfather of America's cuisine, the great James Beard, himself an Oregon native and one of the most influential food writers of the last century in the USA.

The Oregon white (*Tuber gibbosum*)
This develops in symbiosis with fir, pine, oak, hazel, hickory, birch and beech, but it's not found on maple, possibly because the sap inhibits the formation of the mychorrhizae. It's fairly common in the Pacific North-west,

to the west of the Cascade mountains from British Colombia to California. Opinions vary as to whether it smells and tastes as good as its European relatives, and it's generally agreed to be closer to the robust Périgord black (*Tuber melanosporum*) than the more delicate Piedmont white (*T. magnatum*). There is also considerable difference between one truffle and another – possibly because of variations in the species. In the USA, however, locally grown is more likely to mean fresh, an important factor with every truffle.

An autumn-fruiting truffle, the Oregon white is at its best in October and November – gatherers say you'll find it as soon as the above-ground mushrooms start to collapse. It forms 8-10cm (3-4in) below the surface of the forest floor between 10 to 14 days after heavy rain. Its natural predators, in the absence of a native pig – the original truffle-hound of Europe – are the grey squirrel and the chipmunk, both of which dig it up, gobble it down and serve as the main dispersers of its spores. Dogs are not used in the USA; gatherers rake over the leaf-mould to uncover the characteristic bumps, a method which can sometimes result in the appearance in the market-place of immature truffles that haven't yet developed their fragrance.

A medium-sized truffle – usually about the size of an egg – its *peridium*, which is tender (as with the Piedmont white) rather than firm (as with the black varieties), varies from pale ivory to reddish brown to dark chocolate, with a paler interior mottled with veining. The fragrance of a fresh Oregon white, though lacking the Parmesan-garlic hit of "*magnato*", has the same effect on a roomful of people when unpacked in public as the great European truffles. American truffle expert Tanith Tyrr explains the appeal: "Straightfoward and powerful, the cultivated [Oregon] white truffle is the dark, rich essence of pure earth and potent, tangy musk." It holds up well in cooking: so use it in recipes that suit the Périgord black (see pages 84-97).

In Australia, where it's known as the American truffle, it's found in association with eucalyptus, the species endemic to the region.

The Oregon black

Leucangium carthusiana is a large truffle, less common than the Oregon white – usually about the size of a golf-ball – which comes into season from September to March. It is very variable; there's talk of separate species. It has

Truffle hunting in Oregon. The hunters may dress differently, but the prize is much the same.

a tender *peridium*, brown to deep chocolate, and a tan to brown *glebum*, with paler veining. Some say the fragrance is light and others say that it's heavy, but all agree that the over-riding message is pineapple, port, earthiness and chocolate. Use raw or only lightly cooked, as for "*magnato*" (see pages 130–141). It is good, says Larry Evans of the Western Montana Truffle Association, shaved over a creamy potato and leek soup.

Lesser North American truffles and other fungi

These include the Pecan or Texas truffle, *Tuber lyonii* (reclassified from *T. texense*) – the name comes from the pecan orchards in which it was first identified – which is very widespread and found on the West Coast from New Mexico to the Gulf Coast and on the eastern seaboard from the Great Lakes to eastern Canada.

The truffles of Montana are given good reviews by local fungi-fanciers: finds of the edible *Ascomycete barssia* (not strictly a truffle, but treated as such for culinary purposes) have been recorded in July and January under Douglas fir.

Other hypogeous fungi reported as edible and good are members of the *Rhizopogon* species, particularly *R. rubescens*, and *Melanogaster tuberiformus*, a strong-smelling fungi to be used in moderation. *Gautieria monticola*, the skunk truffle, a species which smells strongly of rotting onions, is considered something of an acquired taste!

DESERT TRUFFLES

The truffles of Arabia, which develop underground in the desert, are very varied. They are, in the main, an opportunist crop which appears in the desert after rain, and is eaten by pastoralists and camel-drovers. Philip Iddison explains that they are usually found in close proximity to rock-roses, members of the *Cistus* family, including *Helianthemum lippii*, *H. salicifolium* and *H. ledifolium*. For the benefit of botanists, he continues, the Arabic names for these plants are *hashma*, *khudhr*, *rugrug*, *jaraid*, *jaraid ach-chima* and *jerait* — "all important grazing-plants for animals, including camels, as they continue the fodder supply after the spring annuals have died back."

The desert truffles which come to Middle Eastern markets — often sold by word of mouth from the back of a pick-up truck — are mostly of the robust potato-like *Terfezia* and *Tirmania* species, though *Tuber* species are also found. *Terfezia* are very sandy — when you buy them, you'll be told to chop them before rinsing to allow as much sand as possible to be washed away. The colour ranges from milky coffee to walnut and, like potatoes, these truffles are roundish, with bumps and lobes. They vary in size from as small as a hazelnut to as large as a hen's egg, though some can grow to the size of a canteloup melon. The texture is firm but spongy and they are, say enthusiasts, prone to induce flatulence — a small price to pay for such pleasure. The scent is so faint as to be imperceptible. In the Oman, says Iddison, they are boiled and dressed with a sauteed onion, garlic and tomato sauce flavoured with the spices used for meat dishes. Maxime Rodinson, in *Récherches sur les documents arabes rélatifs à la cuisine* (Paris, 1950), describes the use of Arabic black desert truffles in dishes prepared with eggs, meat and aromatics.

Recent research suggests that some of the desert truffles enjoyed in Greece and Rome in classical times might conceivably have been of the "true" truffle type — members of the *Tuber* species, of which the two found in modern

Turkish markets are *T. micheli* and *T. brumale* — though these are also, somewhat confusingly, called *keme*. Iddison describes them as found in the market in Gaziantep in May, where they are gathered in the pistachio orchards that surround the town: "Covered in fine mud, when brushed and washed, they reavealed a roughish dark brown skin. The consistency was firm, the skin thin and they sliced cleanly to reveal orangy-pink marbled flesh. They had a good nutty texture reminiscent of almonds. The skins were a little tough and research recommended abrading the skin before grilling."

Botanical information on the varieties sold under the name of desert truffles is sparse and hard to check, since they usually eaten as soon as found. *Tirmania nivea,* an autumn truffle, is found in Kuwait where the common name is "*fuga*". *T. nivea* is recorded by Iddison as being on sale in Baghdad, where the common name is *kamaa, kima* or *chima*: "They were a seasonal luxury food in Iraq and served peeled and either boiled or sautéed", rather than, as Paula Wolfert describes in Morocco and Iddison in Oman, being combined with other ingredients. They can be purchased in tins in Middle Eastern delicatessens, though the flavour and texture, says Lebanese food-writer Anissa Helou, is not a patch on the real thing.

RECIPES FOR OTHER TRUFFLES

TRUFFLE BUTTER

This is a good method of preserving secondary black truffles, peelings from "*melano*" or the secondary Italian white, the spring-fruiting "*bianchetto*". Do it quickly, as soon as you've decided not to eat your truffles absolutely fresh. Simply grate 1 part truffle into 3 parts unsalted butter, pot up and freeze. Store in the freezer till you're ready to use it. Delicious on baked potatoes, to finish a risotto, or simply to toss with the pasta.

TRUFFLE BRANDY

Chop up the truffle, use peelings or leave the truffle whole, and pop into a sterilized jam-jar and cover with brandy. Use in gravies, to add a truffle fragrance when you deglaze the frying pan to make a little sauce for steak or anything pan-seared. It keeps indefinitely – well, for a least a year. You can top up the brandy if you wish.

Oregon white truffles: local produce on show at a fair in North America.

LAMB TAGINE WITH TRUFFLES

A lamb tagine flavoured with truffles, says Paula Wolfert in *Good Food from Morocco*, is a typical Moroccan-Jewish speciality; this is a lamb tagine flavoured with carrots and celery, preserved lemons and onions, and finished with white truffles. (In tins, look for the Aicha brand.)

SERVES 4-6

500g (1lb) desert truffles, fresh or tinned

THE COUSCOUS

500g (1lb) couscous grains
1 litre (1¾ pints) vegetable stock or plain water
1 teaspoon powdered saffron or turmeric
Small bunch coriander or parsley sprigs
1 smallish piece cinnamon
1 garlic clove, crushed with salt
1 teaspoon powdered cumin

THE TAGINE

2 tablespoons olive oil
350g (12oz) stewing lamb, diced small
500g (lb) shallots, peeled (quartered lengthways if large, left whole if small)
2 tablespoons raisins
500g (1lb) cooked chickpeas, drained
500g (1lb) potatoes or turnips, peeled and chunked
500g (1lb) carrots, scraped and chunked
1 whole head celery, rinsed and chopped (including the green)
1 preserved lemon, skin only, chopped

HARISSA

1 teaspoon dried red chillies, soaked in hot water
1 clove garlic, skinned
1 teaspoon salt
2 tablespoons olive oil
½ lemon (juice only)
½ teaspoon powdered cumin

If using fresh desert truffles, rinse thoroughly, chop into bite-sized pieces and rinse again to remove all the sand. From a can, drain the truffles, rinse twice, cut into bite-sized pieces and set them aside to add 5 mins before serving.

Soak the couscous grains in cold water for 10 minutes, and then drain off excess water. Work the grains with your fingers to get rid of lumps. Bring the stock or water with its flavourings to the boil in a large saucepan (with a steamer). Line the steamer with a piece of clean muslin or linen and put in the couscous. Set it over the boiling stock and steam for 20 minutes, uncovered. Remove and tip the couscous out onto a wide surface. Sprinkle with cold water and work out any lumps, then return it to the steamer.

Heat the oil in a frying pan and add the lamb and onions, turning until lightly browned all over. Drop the contents of the pan into the boiling stock and add the truffles (if fresh), raisins, potatoes or turnips, carrots and preserved lemon. Bring all back to the boil and cook for another 10 minutes. Add the celery and preserved lemon and continue to cook for the final 10 minutes, until the vegetables are tender. If using canned truffles, add them now 5 minutes before the end of cooking.

Meanwhile, drop the harissa ingredients in the liquidizer with a ladleful of the vegetable broth, and process to a puree. Reheat to serve — in Morocco you can get a tiny earthenware brazier to keep the sauce hot. Serve the couscous piled high on a hot serving-dish, with the vegetables prettily arranged on top and plenty of liquor to moisten. Serve the harissa sauce separately.

Cultivating truffles

The following offers some basic information on truffle farming, on the conditions required for growing truffles successfully, and on the principles of truffle husbandry.

HISTORY OF TRUFFICULTURE

The first attempts at truffle cultivation were in France in 1756, when truffles were sown in open fields by the naturalist Georges Buffon, Keeper of the King's Botanical Garden and author of *Histoire Naturel,* a monumental and highly influential work on the natural history of the planet, which ran to thirty-six volumes. However, since there were no host trees available, the initial experiment failed.

Shortly afterwards, by accident, success was achieved by the Procurator-General of the regional assembly of Aix-en-Provence, who planted oaks on his land at Bourgane, St. Saturnin les Apt: ten years later, truffles were harvested. More plantations followed: in Mauléon in 1790 in the departement of Vienne, and in Talon in 1810 in the Vaucluse. Some 40 years later, Rousseau, a truffle

A newly planted truffle plantation. The trees are spaced to allow the precise requirements for shade and sunlight that truffles require.

trader from Carpentras, spread the word on trufficulture — his message, essentially, was: if you want truffles, plant sapplings — during the course of the Great Exhibition in Paris in 1855, but the jury denied him recognition and medals on the grounds that trufficulture was too speculative ever to achieve universal acceptance. Pioneering trufficulturists persevered. In 1869, the École Supérieure de Pharmacie in Paris registered, under the guidance of Professor Chatin, Head of Botany, 54 departments of France as truffle producing. At this time, production of the Périgord truffle from unimproved (natural) woodland was estimated to be between 1,000 and 2,000 tonnes. Compare this with the 20-40 tonnes gathered annually in modern times, including produdction from managed or specially planted woodlands, and it must be supposed that the decline is owing to loss of expertise as well as loss of habitat.

The late 1800s were a time well suited to the truffle. Reforestation following a period of decline — marginal land abandoned during the drift to the towns, the ravages of *philoxera* causing people to abandon or grub up their vineyards — led to large areas of light cover, open woodland with trees and bushes of varying heights, perfect terrain for the truffle. Meanwhile, unfortunately, much of the expertise needed to crop the woodland was being lost through depopulation. And since trufficulture was not yet a proven technique, the woodlands proceeded to climax — and climax woodland, lacking air and sunlight, is a habitat in which the truffle cannot thrive. The process continued throughout the two world wars, dropping first to 500 tonnes between the wars, and to 100 tonnes at the end of World War Two.

When, in the middle of the 20th century, agronomists first turned their attention to actively restoring truffle woodland, the process which would lead to regeneration was little understood and its complexity underestimated. One consequence was the moving of truffle plantations from terrain which suited them — marginal land, stony, steep, well-drained — to the richer pastures of the valley floor, where the soil was far less suitable — too rich, wet, fertile and over-pesticided. Laboratory research led to the production of mycorrhized rootstock in 1974, and modern science-based trufficulture began to pay dividends. In 2004, production from France's truffle orchards, although improving to the above mentioned 20-40 tonnes of *Tuber melanosporum* and 7 tonnes of *T. uncinatum*, are nowhere near enough to satisfy the market. French production provides between a half and a third of the total production of the Périgord black, the other main producers being Spain and Italy. With the loss of knowledge in the countryside, truffle orchards – inseminated trees tended and irrigated – are increasingly seen as the only way to ensure future supplies.

HOW THE TRUFFLE GROWS

The first phase in the growth of a truffle is conception – the development of a fruiting body on the mycelium. For *Tuber melanosporum* this happens in October and November and the crucial growth-time is December and January. For *"magnato"* conception happens in June and July and the crucial growth-time is between September and October. There must be sufficient warmth and rainfall to bring a truffle to maturity. Usually a root yields one truffle a year, though twins are possible. After cropping, it's important to restore the habitat as closely as possible to its former state. Truffles tend to grow in the same place year after year and they won't germinate if the soil has been disturbed and the roots broken or left exposed.

Food-and-travel writer Burton Anderson explains its lifecycle as follows: "A spore from a previous year's truffle germinates into an embryo fungus, whose vegetative part, or mycelium, consists of thread-like filaments called *hyphae*. These attach themselves to tree roots, whose sap nourishes the parasitical truffle in a symbiosis known as mycorrhiza. The formation of the fruiting body, the truffle, occurs only when conditions of humidity and temperature are right."

The subterranean environment – the nature of the soil – dictates which truffle species will find it attractive. For all species, the soil must be porous enough for oxygen to reach the fruiting-body, though this can be achieved in different ways. *Tuber magnatum*, for instance, likes damp clay of the kind which suits the potter's wheel – lightly alkaline, calcereous or siliceous – and attracts or is attracted by the undergrown tunnels made by hibernating snails, creatures which also enjoy the truffle as a snack, leaving little nibble-marks on its surface. Rocky terrain rich in minerals rarely produces truffles of any kind. Truffles appreciate the same conditions enjoyed by other fungi: Alba, for instance, also has good crops of porcini and in the Périgord the truffle merchant in the market often has other locally gathered fungi – chanterelles, pieds de mouton, trompettes de la mort – on sale as well. In Piedmont, the best are generally agreed to come from Roero, which has a higher than usual proportion of sand in the soil. In the Langhe, they'll tell you that the compact clay which produces intensely delicious wines also produces the best truffles.

HINTS ON CULTIVATION

Black truffles (*Tuber melanosporum, T. aestivum, T. uncinatum*)
Under the microscope at the trufficulture laboratory at Sant'Angelo-in-Vado, Italy, the mycelium on the little trees is visible as a spider's web of fine filaments, with the infant fungi like little golden bulbs on the ends of the hairy-fine roots. "Look here — at the tip of the knife."

There they are, the *tartufo nero di Norcia*, as the Italians call them, the *truffes Périgourdines* as they're known in France, or, in the laboratory, "*melano*", to distinguish them clearly from other varieties. Such is the care and attention lavished on all esteemed varieties of truffle, both white and black, the future of the species seems assured. Even if this is in semi-cultivation, the truffle remains in essence a wild crop, random, following its own agenda. "While with the main varieties of the black — "*melano*" and *Tuber aestivum* — we can expect a strike-rate of around 75 per cent after 7 to 10 years, the white needs at least 20 years and the strike-rate has until now been too low to count. And even if you're successful, you need a dog. The white leaves no imprint — what the French called the *brulée* — round the tree and there's no little fly to tell you where to look. It's also very localized. In the wild, it shares the territory with all the lesser varieties though it's almost never in direct competition — a situation which means you can get cross-overs — lesser varieties which rush in and take advantage of the territory you've created. If the terrain is not perfect and the host-tree reluctant, you'll get a crop of something you don't want. It's a risky business."

The first step in producing mycorrhized trees under laboratory conditions is the sterilization of the soil in the pots in which the seedlings are to be sprouted: the danger of infection with rival mycorrhizal fungi — *Tuber brumale, T. uncinatum, T. aestivum* or even unidentified others — continues throughout the growth cycle in the greenhouse as well as the plantation. Oak and hazel are the usual vehicles, with the latter favoured for speed of growth and the former for length of time in production and quality of truffle. In France and Italy, the holm or evergreen

Truffle cultivation in France — the two-year-old green truffle oaks ready for planting out.

oak, ilex or pubescent oak and the prickly leaved kermes oak (*Quercus pubescense, Q. ilex, Q. coccifera* respectively*)* are the main sources in the wild, with lime, poplar and hazel as secondary ones. Occasional producers include the ash tree and the Aleppo pine, though its truffles are said to be a little resinous. Rock-roses — members of the *Cistus* family — are credited with producing them in Spain, though opinions differ as to whether this is so. Of all these potential hosts, kermes oak and hazel are proving the most adaptable to greenhouse conditions.

Trees — both planted and in the wild — are variable in their capacity to produce. One truffle-tree ranked as of high productivity will produce between 1 to 3kg (2-7lb) truffles a year; a tree of middling productivity will deliver 200-500g (½ to 1lb) a year; a tree of low productivity is best replaced with another. A hectare (2.5 acres) of well-tended truffle woodland, whether natural or artificial, in an average year for rainfall and under reasonable weather conditions, will produce 5-20kg (11-44lb) truffles. While no-one can guarantee the productivity of a plantation even when all conditions are fulfilled, once a tree comes into production the probability is it will continue to produce. As a rough rule of thumb, a good year for wine will be a bad year for truffles, and visa versa.

Tuber melanosporum takes a month to six weeks to ripen, a generous window of opportunity during which it can be found by a predator – pig, dog or human. As it ripens, the fragrance becomes more powerful before finally, if undiscovered, tipping into rottenness – a process which transforms the delicate fragrance into the stench of petroleum and the meat into a soft, inedible mass of powdery spores.

In France, information from the Languedoc-Roussillon, where much of the experimental work is being carried out, a century and a half after trufficulture experiments were initiated under laboratory conditions, indicates progress is moving away from artificial orchard-production and towards management of existing woodlands in areas suitable for truffles. Truffle woodlands – as distinct from purpose-planted truffle orchards – can be established wherever conditions are right – chalky soil, sufficient irrigation, suitable hosts – by managing the woodland in order to maintain it at optimum level by encouraging what is already there as well as introducing laboratory-mycorrhyzed saplings. The work requires careful monitoring of the terrain both before and during the production-cycle – for this you need the help of a well-trained truffle-hound – and management in the form of felling and replanting to keep the woodlands productive.

In areas that already produce truffles, the task is to restore previously productive woodlands and maintain the health of truffle plantations which have been allowed to fall into non-productivity. These activities can take place in large areas where the prospects of success are correspondingly greater, though these are rarely available, or in micro-zones, small areas that can be carefully monitored and husbanded. Income that becomes available from non-truffle sources in truffle woodland is from wood for carpentry and firewood, and from other fungi – boleti, chanterelles. Recreational activities related to tourism include fungi and truffle forays, a reliable source of income in the season.

Nowadays, with the laboratory dictating many of the choices that guarantee its survival, traditional methods of gathering are also under review. The business has been international for at least twenty years, with funding coming from the multinational enterprises which the create world markets that set the price of all but the most locally appreciated of foodstuffs. So it might come as no surprise that it was an article in the *Knaresborough Post* which revealed (in 1990) that a certain Mr. John Sonly had, in response to a request from a biochemist studying truffle vapours for his doctoral thesis at Toulouse, developed a gas-detecting device which would take over the duties of the truffle dog in the woods of the Périgord. This, it was clearly stated, was only intended as a last resort at the end of the day when the animal was tired from its exertions – not as a substitute. "Mr. Talou," the inventor explained, "asked me to find an electronic nose, not to actually replace the dogs and pigs, but because they tire very quickly. However," he added, "having visited him and seen the dogs in operation, I don't think anything could replace them."

The Piedmont white

Cultivation of *Tuber magnato* is still in its infancy. Host trees (*piante madri*) capable of supporting "*magnato*" are oak, producer of dense-fleshed highly fragrant truffles with a deep colour; linden – *tilleul* or lime tree – which delivers truffles with the strongest aroma of all, though this is short-lived; poplar and willow produce less aromatic truffles, while pine is host to the spring-fruiting "*bianchetto*" (*Tuber borchii*).

The white's specific needs are a thin, soft layer of soil along with a good circulation of air, a combination rarely found in nature. It also needs the correct balance of rainfall at a time of year which suits its pattern of development. In the Roero district of Piedmont, a rocky region bordering on the Langhe, the necessary porous layer is formed during the autumn rains of the previous year which produce fast, local flooding of the rivers across the valley floors, and form a porous layer of new soil in spring for colonization by the mycohrriza; this must be followed by a cool, damp summer. The cycle has to be annually renewed since the soil naturally compacts and loses its porosity as a result of the firming effect of new vegetation, mainly grass. A variety of seemingly different habitats are capable of producing soils which suit it. Natural truffle grounds are formed by shifting conditions which must be annually renewed by minor surface landslides, a regular occurence down the entire length of the Appenines, from Emiglia Romagna as far as the mountainous areas of southern Italy. Sometimes a freeze followed by a thaw can produce the right conditions by forming a porous layer of soil, such as that found around Mugello and Montefeltro. Sometimes the appropriate conditions can be inadvertently created by shallow tilling of arable land. The three basic requirements – quality and texture of soil, presence of appropriate host-trees, degree and timing of temperature and rainfall – must all be present for the mycelium to fruit.

Since "*magnato*" is the least flexible and most locality-specific of the valuable truffles — confined to certain areas of northern Italy, the north-eastern corner of the former Yugoslavia and a patch of southern Switzerland — even limited success is welcome, though it is expected it will be several years before the trees will be supplied commercially, and even then plantings will be confined to existing "*magnato*"-friendly areas. The agrobotanists at the biological station at Sant'Angelo-in-Vado have long experience of the difficulties of producing "*magnato*" as a crop. The problem, they say, is not the actual mycorrhization, which is much the same for all varieties of truffle, but the creation of a suitable habitat. The white is far more demanding of terrain, host and subsidiary plantings than any other variety. "The white has a very

complex ecosystem which is hard to replicate. It likes shade and there must be bushes as well as trees. It's a very delicate balance, even for those who have the resources of the laboratory at their fingertips – and we've been working on it for years. This year for the first time we've had a few calls, nothing dramatic – we're talking two to three out of a hundred clients who've planted experimental trees. But it's a start."

Even the most careful artificial mycorrhization does not necessarily produce results. The first phase – conception – happens in June and July, but the crucial time is between September and October, the period of growth before the fruiting body comes to maturity. Each mycelium produces one truffle a year, further limiting its viability as a crop. The rate of ripening for "*magnato*" is between a single day and a week, offering a very short time in which the fragrance is discernible, the only indication, that the crop can be harvested. Rain in June is the best promise of a good crop, say the *trifolaos* of Alba. Late rain is not so desirable, though dampness is essential for the truffle to fruit. "When the earth is dry the truffles hide." The main enemies of "*magnato*", say the gatherers, are not so much loss of habitat as chemicals in the ground, pollution and industrial smog, since they are often found very close to the road. Each mycelium produces one truffle a year, further limiting viability as a crop.

The basic soil requirements – chalky clay with silica – are found in the Monferrato and Alba regions, where the fruiting body develops at a depth of between 10-35cm (4-14in), deeper than other truffles, which may possibly account for the lack of *brulée*. "*Magnato*" truffles which associate with oaks, are darker in colour and have a stronger scent than those which associate with limetrees, which produce truffles that are lighter in colour and more delicate in fragrance. White truffles which grow in association with poplars – colonizers of loosely packed soil by riverbanks – are rounder, whiter and smoother on the outside, but the fragrance is not so distinguished. Soft ground produces a rounded and regular form, while compact soil leaves its print by producing an irregular, lumpy form, since the tuber has to struggle for growth. The terrain must also be subject to minor movement – such as landslips, the indirect action of the plough, even the movement of earth when roads are being built nearby.

The hilly slopes of Piedmont, the heartland of the Italian white truffle.

Truffle plantations around the world

In the USA, the largest plantations are in Texas and Oregon. Although truffles are harvested in both places, the largest European importer-exporter – Urbani of Norcia, who control 65 per cent of the world's trade in both the black and the white – said at the time of writing that they are not so far of a quality to be of interest.

In Asia, the Chinese truffle (*Tuber sinensis*) found in quantity in the wild at high altitude in the provinces of Szechuan and Hunan, usually on pine and a local species of oak, *Quercus incana*, is said to be in cultivation, though information is sparse.

In North America, truffle plantations have been established for decades, though most of the production is absorbed by local markets – mainly sold directly to restaurant chefs. Areas of production include North Carolina, where a hundred infected trees are recorded as producing around 20kg (44lb) of "*melano*" per annum, and to the north of Santa Rosa, California, where 400 seedlings (from Umbria) produce regular harvest of 27 to 45kg (60-100lb). Most notable, however, is a large plantation in Texas, at Hext, about 100 miles north-west of Austin, where 60,000 mycorrhized hazelnuts (*Corylus* sp.) were planted in 1992 in rolling hill country aided by controlled irrigation systems: here, truffles began to appear in the year 2000, though quality is still under assessment. The growers use trained dogs to detect the fungi, as in Europe.

There are high hopes of truffles from the Antipodes, in areas where latitude mirrors that of the European truffle areas – notably New Zealand and Tasmania – in anticipation that, with the reversal of seasons, crops will come into the market at times when the northern truffles are not available. There have, however, been problems with cross-fertilization with lesser species which has kept market-availablity low. The crop is still locally absorbed, so comparisons and success-rates are hard to quantify.

In Britain, Nigel Hadden-Paton has had success with mycorrhization of the Périgord black (*Tuber melanospermum*), supplying treated trees to would-be planters in areas where the terrain is suitable. In Britain, only *T. aestivum*-infected trees are so far considered a possibility for transplanting, though this, he says, may change. A farmer in Herefordshire, he came to the conclusion that truffle production might be a possibility when he was looking at alternative crops . "I started looking at truffles because I knew they'd been doing it successfully in other parts of the world. There's huge scepticism about the technology. Nobody knows why and exactly how the chemistry works. New Zealand has the right climate – it sits across a similar latitude to the Périgord, but in the southern hemisphere. And Tasmania has been successful in a limited way. We acquired the technology ourselves in 2001, when I sold the farm and moved down to Somerset to set up my own facilities with greenhouses for germination. We're now producing trees infected with *T. melanosporum* as well as *T. aestivum* and *T. uncinatum*. The last two are scientifically identical although the French swear there is a difference."

And the future? Tasmania is indeed a success story, though localized, with production from a single plantation making its way to the smart restaurants of Sydney and Melbourne. As a general rule of thumb, terrain that suits a winemaker is also likely to provide a habitat for truffle producers. And it may well be that future generations of farmers will discover what French vineyard-owners have long believed, that gastronomy's two most glamorous partners – wine and truffles – thrive in each other's company.

Management of truffle plantations

Although truffle plantation management is a matter of what works in the area in which you find yourself – truffle plantations in Tasmania do not necessarily provide a blueprint for truffle plantations in New Zealand – certain general rules apply. Experience in Languedoc-Roussillon in southern France has provided much of the detailed information available for *Tuber melanosporum,* the only one of the two high-value species for which the success-rate is high enough to make the exercise commercially viable.

In a two-part series in *Fôret-Entreprise* (August and December 2004) ecologist Alban Lauriac provided France's foresters with an up-to-date account of work in progress. His recommendations on the care of truffle plantantions are from first-hand experience in the region – Languedoc-Roussillon – and he is careful to point out the benefits of woodland management for truffles as a contribution to the general health of local ecosystems – encouraging respect for the environment as well as providing a source of hardwood, a crop in short supply throughout the world.

His advice, in summary, is that managed woodland dictates its own agenda – no substitute like knowing your own trees. In general, gardening exercises such as thinning and clearing of undergrowth should take place on a three-year cycle: the aim is to create gaps in the canopy to allow light and air to reach the roots of productive trees. The root-systems of truffle-producing trees should be as widespread and vigorous as possible: trees whose growth is no longer vigorous should be cropped. Thinning should be for the benefit of productive trees, after careful assessment of individual woodlands while taking into account climate-conditions and degree of exposure. First thinnings should be of non-host trees, followed by host-trees of weak growth. With fast-growing trees, thinning is done in early summer in order to minimize regrowth, avoiding the destruction of the phytocydes, the nodules that appear at conception and act as exchange-points for mycorrhization.

Coppicing, useful for reviving a tree which has fallen out of production for a few years, can also be used to encourage a non-productive host-tree. This work should be carried out in March or November, the most suitable time to encourage regrowth of the roots. Seedlings which appear in situ are preferable to new plantings. Production of *Tuber melanosporum* and *T. aestivum* can be maintained as long as the woodland is kept at parkland level – a matter of spacing – and not allowed to escalate to forest-cover. Shade-cover should be no more than 10 per cent of the total surface. If the climate is Mediterranean or the terrain is south-facing and low-altitude, a deep cover of loam is required, particularly if productivity is already established. If the situation is north-facing or the altitude is high, less cover is advisable, particularly if the plantation is not yet productive. In France, *T. melanosporum* usually appears in the patch of shade created by the tree in the afternoon – the north-east. It may be possible to extend the productive patch – the *brulée* – by leaving the vegetation to the south-west of the tree undisturbed.

All this, of course, applies to conditions in the Languedoc. The best advice, meanwhile, is if you want to invest in the technology, make sure you know your terrain. Restoring the essential elements of wildwood lost over many generations improves the health of the planet and, for those who want their legacy to make a difference to their grandchildren, that may be reward enough.

You have asked the scholars what this tubercle is, and after two thousand years of discussion, the scholars have answered the same as the first day: "We do not know." You have asked the truffle itself and the truffle has answered you: "Eat me and adore God." To tell the story of the truffle is to tell the history of the world's civilization. Alexandre Dumas, *Le Grand Dictionnaire de Cuisine* (Paris, 1873).

USEFUL INFORMATION

ALBA Epicentre of the world for "*magnato Pico*".

ALBA POMPEIA Heartland of the Piedmont truffle.

ALBANIA A source of imported (and, by definition, inferior) truffles.

ANDROSTENOL A chemical, the active ingredient in the pheromones which produce the scent which attracts the pig to the truffle.

ASTI (see also Alba) Second most famous place in the world for *Tuber magnato*.

BASTARDELLI DI PAGLIO "Haystack" mongrels of the type used as truffle hounds in Italy.

BRACCIONIERI Poachers of Italian truffles.

BRULÉE Literally, French for burned: a circular patch formed around a tree affected by the mycorrhizae of *Tuber melanosporum*. The hyphae spread themselves all around the root system, producing a protective apron of antibiotic-drenched soil as a defence against disease-carrying micro-organisms. Now you know it all.

CARBOHYDRATES Food provided from the truffle host-tree via photosynthesis to the truffle, enabling it to grow.

CHINESE TRUFFLES For information go to www.chengduhuakai.com

CROATIAN TRUFFLES For information go to info@zigante-tartufi.de

ECTOMYCORRHIZAE The web of filaments which form in association with certain trees.

FOREST DESTRUCTION The main reason for disappearance of the truffle.

GLEBA Flesh or pulp of the truffle.

HYPHAE Gossamer-fine filaments emitted by the mycorrhizae, the symbiotic organs (under the microscope, they look like tiny light-bulbs) which develop on the tree's hair-like outer roots; the non-fruiting part of the fungi which helps absorb minerals on behalf of the tree.

MYCELIUM Fine web of filaments that form the support-system for the fruiting body, the truffle. Each mycelium produces one truffle a year.

MYCORRHIZATION The process of infecting the roots of a host-tree with the symbiotic fungus.

NEBBIA Morning mist in the valleys of the Langhe hills (Italy).

OMERTA The silence which applies to those dealing in truffles (Italy).

PERIDIUM Rind or skin – the outer covering of a truffle.

PERIGUEUX Epicentre of the world for *Tuber melanosporum*.

PHEROMONE A substance secreted in the testicles and saliva of, among others, the male pig, including wild boar, men's armpits, women's urine, certain members of the cabbage family and, to a greater or lesser extent, all varieties of truffle.

PIANTE MADRI Italian for host-tree, notably oak, hazel, lime, poplar, willow, pine.

PICO The Italian botanist who first identified *Tuber magnato*, the magnate's truffle.

RAMASSEUR French term for truffle hunter.

SAPIN French term for little pickaxe-spade for digging up truffles.

SYMBIOSIS Interdependence between species.

TAJARIN SIENESE Narrow ribbons of all-egg pasta eaten with white truffle.

TARTUFFE Moliere's deceitful hero of his most famous play.

TARTUFO Truffle (Italy).

TERFEZ Generic name for Arabian desert truffles of the Terfezia species, popular in throughout the Middle East, found from Turkey to Morocco, including the Sinai desert. Eaten by the Romans with garum, a salty fermented-fish preparation much like anchovy essence. Used in Jewish cooking, flavoured with *ras-al-hanout*, a spice mix of which the main component is coriander.

TRICASTIN Major truffle-producing region in France – an upland area of Provence, roughly triangular, between Montelimar, Orange and Nyons, which was awarded a protective denomination of origin (DOC): *Truffe noire de Tricastin*, in 1978.

TRIFOLAO Italian dialect for truffle gatherer.

TRUFA Spanish and Portuguese for truffle.

TRUFFE French for truffle.

TRUFFLE FLY An indicator of the presence of black truffles (though not of the white), a small reddish fly which lays its eggs on ripe truffles. The best time for fly-spotting is between 11am and 4pm. The method traditionally used for hunting by fly is to sweep the ground in likely areas with a hazel twig and watch for the fly to rise. It never goes far and always returns to the spot of interest, pin-pointing it with greater accuracy. Silence must be observed throughout.

TRUFOLA Piedmont dialect for truffle.

TUBER AESTIVUM Lesser species, but prized as a background flavouring, a summer-maturing truffle found in all truffle-producing territories. Also known as the English truffle and the *truffe de St. Jean*, the midsummer truffle. Mentioned by John Evelyn in *Acetaria* and still found in considerable quantities in the wild in southern England.

TUBER BORCHII Lesser white truffle which comes to maturity in the spring, known and valued in Italy as the *"bianchetto"*.

TUBER GIBBOSUM The Oregon white truffle, prized in the USA, particularly in its own territory.

TUBER INDICUM, T. SINENSIS, T. HIMALAYENSIS The Chinese black. An inferior truffle – lacks fragrance and texture – though cheap and imported in large quantities to augment supplies of European truffles. No record of culinary use in China, though used medicinally.

TUBER MAGNATO The Piedmont white, also known as the magnate's truffle, prized in Italy above all others.

TUBER MELANOSPORUM The Perigord black truffle, prized in France above all others, and also in Italy, in the region of Norcia in the province of Umbria.

TUBER TEXENSE, T. CANALICULATUM Lesser truffles prized in their own territories – northern USA and southern Canada.

TUBER UNCINATUM, T. BRUMALE Inferior black truffles.

BIBLIOGRAPHY

Further reading and books mentioned in the text:

Allende, Isabel *Afrodita* (Plaza y Janas, Madrid. 1997)

Anderson, Burton *Pleasures of the Italian Table* (Penguin, 1995)

Baietta, Cristiana (ed) *The Italian Truffle Guide* (Touring Club Italiano, 2001)

Bentley, James *Life and Food in the Dordogne* (Weidenfeld, 1987)

Black, William *Al Dente* (Bantam, 2003)

Callot, Gabriel (gen. ed.) *La truffe, la terre, la vie* (INRA editions, 1999)

Colette, Sidonie-Gabrielle *Prisons et Paradis* (Fayard)

del Conte, Ana *A Gastronomy of Italy* (Bantam 1987)

Dubary, Francoise & Sabine Bacquet-Grenet, *L'Abcdaire de la Truffe* (Flammarion, 2001)

Dumas, Alexandre *Le Grand Dictionnaire de Cuisine* (Paris, 1873)

Evelyn, John *Acetaria* (London, 1699)

Fisher, Mary Frances Kennedy *Two Towns in Provence* (Vintage, 1983)

Freedman, Louise *Wild about Mushrooms* (Aris Books, 1987)

Hall, Ian & Gordon Brown & James Byars *The Black Truffle: its history, uses and cultivation* (Crop and Food Research, Christchurch, New Zealand 1994)

Lauriac, Alban *Sous les fôrets, la truffe* (Foret-entreprise 158/160, Languedoc-Roussillon, 2004)

Manelfi, Giovanni *Mensa romana* (Rome, 1650)

Martin, Neil A Neuroanatomy of Flavour (Petits Propos Culinaires, 2004)

Osler, Mirabel *The Elusive Truffle* (Pavilion, 1996)

Pebeyre, Pierre-Jean & Jacques *Le Grand Livre de la Truffe* (Editions Daniel Brand Robert Laffont, 1988)

Peterson, Sarah *Acquired Taste, The French Origins of Modern Cooking* (Cornell UP, 1994)

Phillips, Roger A series of excellent fungi identification manuals (Pan) and a website, www.rogersmushroms. com

Platina *De honesta voluptate* (Rome, 17th century)

Renoy, Georges & Luigi Ciciriello *Truffles from the Heart* (Les Editions de la Truffe Noire, 1999)

Rocchia, Michel *Truffles: the Black Diamond and other Kinds* (Barthelemy, Avignon, 1992)

Safina, Rosario & Judith Sutton *Truffles, Ultimate Luxury, Everyday Pleasure* (John Wiley & Sons, USA, 2003)

Sitwell, Sacheverell *Truffle Hunt* (Robert Hale, 1953)

Sobin, Gustaf *The Fly-truffler* (Norton, 2000)

Il Tartufo nelle Marche (Guidebook, ed. Regione Marche, 2001)

Toussaint-Samat, Maguelonne *Histoire naturelle et morale de la nourriture* (Paris, 1987).

Tyrr, Tanith *The Truffle FAQ* (Bay Gourmet web page, 1997)

Wolfert, Paula *Good Food in Morocco* (John Murray, revised ed., 1989)

INDEX

AUTHOR'S ACKNOWLEDGMENTS

Acknowledgments are well and truly due for shared feastings as well as practical assistance in the making of this book. For nose-skill, expertise in all things Italian, patience and unlimited hospitality, Nancy Harmon Jenkins in Tuscany and Umbria. For the same in Le Marche, as well as reminiscences of childhood in his home-territory, Franco Taruschio and his wife Ann, the great restaurateurs of Abergavenny. For illumination and a pair of the finest truffles a woman has ever grated over pasta, Olga Urbani, truffle-trader extraordinary of Norcia and Alba. For reminiscences of Arabian desert truffles, the beautiful Anissa Helou. For expertise on forestry and willingness to pursue what it takes to make a tuber grow, my neighbour and professional woodsman, Philippe Morgan. For pointing me in the right direction at the start, Paul Levy and Henrietta Green. For help, information and discreet introductions along the way, mushroom superstar Roger Phillips. For the loan of truffle-territory in the Luberon, artist-painter Anne Dunn. For assistance in keeping up with the modern truffle-business, Nigel Haden Patten and Martin Lewy. For tireless truffle-hounding on the internet, Alex Sapirstein, genius of the mouse. For coming up with the whole seductive idea and keeping the show on the road, editor Susan Berry, photographer John Heseltine, and designer and illustrator Anne Wilson. For getting us all to the finishing line in good order, publisher John Nicoll and in-house editor Jo Christian. And thanks are due, as always, to my agent Abner Stein for looking after me for thirty years, above and beyond the call of duty. May their truffle-baskets never be empty.

PHOTOGRAPHER'S ACKNOWLEDGMENTS

Thanks to the Ayme family at the Domaine de Bramerel and Robert Ytier and the staff at the Hotel St. Ferme, and to all those who generously allowed themselves, or their truffles or truffle hounds, to be photographed. The image on page 42 is courtesy of the Maison de la Truffe et du Tricastin, St. Paul Trois Chateaux.